Towards Democratic Schooling

Innovations in Education

Series Editor: Colin Fletcher (Senior Lecturer in the School of Policy Studies, Cranfield Institute of Technology)

There have been periods of major innovation in public education. What do the achievements amount to and what are the prospects for progress now? There are issues in each slice of the education sector. How have the issues come about?

Each author analyses their own sphere, argues from experience and communicates clearly. Here are books that speak both with and for the teaching profession; books that can be shared with all those involved in the future of education.

Three quotations have helped to shape the series:

The whole process – false starts, frustrations, adaptions, the successive recasting of intentions, the detours and conflicts – needs to be comprehended. Only then can we understand what has been achieved and learn from experience.

Marris and Rein

In this time of considerable educational change and challenge the need for teachers to write has never been greater.

Hargreaves

A wise innovator should prepare packages of programmes and procedures which . . . would be put into effect quickly in periods of recovery and reorganisation following a disaster.

Hirsh

Current titles in the series

Pat Ainley: *From School to YTS*
Garth Allen, John Bastiani, Ian Martin, Kelvyn Richards:
  Community Education
Bernard Barker: *Rescuing the Comprehensive Experience*
Julia Gilkes: *Developing Nursery Education*
Gerri Kirkwood and Colin Kirkwood: *Living Adult Education*
Herbert Kohl: *36 Children*
Julia Stanley: *Marks on the Memory*
Jan Stewart: *The Making of the Primary School*
David Terry: *The Tertiary College*
Paul Widlake: *Reducing Educational Disadvantage*

Towards Democratic Schooling

European Experiences

EDITED BY

Knud Jensen
and Stephen Walker

Open University Press
Milton Keynes · Philadelphia

Open University Press
12 Cofferidge Close
Stony Stratford
Milton Keynes MK11 1BY

and
1900 Frost Road, Suite 101
Bristol, PA19007, USA

First Published 1989
Copyright © The Editors and Contributors 1989

British Library Cataloguing in Publication Data

Towards democratic schooling. – (Innovations
   in education)
   1. Schools. Democracy
   I. Jensen Knud   II. Walker, Stephen *1944–*
   III. Series
   371

   ISBN 0-335-09568-2
   ISBN 0-335-09567-4 (pbk)

Library of Congress Cataloging-in-Publication Data

Towards democratic schooling / edited by Knud Jensen and Stephen
   Walker.
         p.   cm. — (Innovations in education)
      Includes index.
      ISBN 0-335-09568-2   ISBN 0-335-09567-4 (pbk.)
      1. Student government—Europe—Case studies.   I. Jensen, Knud.
   II. Walker, Stephen, 1944– .   III. Series.
   LB3092.TSB   1989   89-3348
   371.5'9'094—dc20   CIP

Photoset by Rowland Phototypesetting Ltd,
Bury St Edmunds, Suffolk
Printed in Great Britain by
Biddles Ltd, Guildford and King's Lynn

Contents

List of contributors

ELIA SERRA PEREIRA DE ALMEIDA, GEP, Ministério da Educação e Cultura, Lisbon, Portugal

COLETTE AUGOYARD, Collège Villeneuve, Grenoble, France

CARL BAGGE, Skolen på Islands Brygge, Copenhagen, Denmark

JEAN BERBAUM, Université de Grenoble II, France

MARIA DO CARMO CLIMACO, GEP, Ministério da Educação e Cultura, Lisbon, Portugal

NILS DANIELSEN, Rosenlundskolen, Skovlunde, Denmark

PIET DECKERS, Stichting Centrum voor Onderwijsonderzoek van de Universiteit van Amsterdam, The Netherlands

MARJA VAN ERP, Stichting Centrum voor Onderwijsonderzoek van de Universiteit van Amsterdam, The Netherlands

COLIN FLETCHER, Cranfield Institute of Technology, Cranfield, Bedfordshire, UK

ELISABETH SPAET HENRIKSEN, The Royal Danish School of Educational Studies, Copenhagen, Denmark

SVEND HESSELHOLDT, The Royal Danish School of Educational Studies, Copenhagen, Denmark

CLAIRE HÜLSENBECK, ABC (Advies en Begeleidingscentrum voor het Onderwijs) Amsterdam, The Netherlands

BERNARD JARDEL, Collège Villeneuve, Grenoble, France

KNUD JENSEN, The Royal Danish School of Educational Studies, Copenhagen, Denmark

HANS JØRGEN KRISTENSEN, N. Zahles College of Education, Denmark

OLE B. LARSEN, The Royal Danish School of Educational Studies, Copenhagen, Denmark

PAT O'SHEA, Peers School, Oxford, UK

HANNE SCHNEIDER, Skolen på Islands Brygge, Copenhagen, Denmark

FREDERIK SMIT, Institute for Social and Behavioural Studies, Katholieke Universiteit, Nijmegen, The Netherlands

TINEKE SMIT, Basisschool de Kinkerhoek, Amsterdam, The Netherlands

SIBE SOUTENDIJK, ABC (Advies en Begeleidingscentrum voor het Onderwijs), Amsterdam, The Netherlands

SUSANNE THURN, Laborschule an der Universität Bielefeld, Bielefeld, Federal Republic of Germany

STEPHEN WALKER, Newman and Westhill Colleges, Birmingham, UK

ELKE WERNEBURG, Universität Bielefeld, Bielefeld, Federal Republic of Germany

Acknowledgements

Many of the ideas presented in this book first found expression at the European Conference Concerning School Democratization held in Gilleleje, October 1987. The conference received financial support from UNESCO and from the Royal Danish School of Educational Studies (RDSES) and was the idea and accomplishment of the four members of the Laboratory of Democratic Educational Research, RDSES, Copenhagen.

As editors, we have a debt to many people. Thanks to Linda Fisher for her help with translation and to Ellie Tagmose and Janet Cowsill for their secretarial work and their cheerful patience. Thanks to the Directorates of RDSES, Copenhagen and of Newman College, Birmingham for financial support in the preparation of this manuscript.

Especial thanks to Lise Jensen and to Sandra Walker.

Preface

For some years now, the Laboratory of Democratic Educational Research at the Royal Danish School of Educational Studies, Copenhagen, has been involved in projects which are inspired by a basic commitment to the process of democratization in schools. In October 1987, the members of the Laboratory brought together teachers and educational researchers from seven European nations to a conference. The conference was designed to provide a forum for sharing experiences of educational innovations which could be defined as progressive or within the sphere of a concern with democratization. The chapters in this collection have come out of this meeting.

The original agenda for the conference identified the following major areas as starting-points for discussion, starting-points in the sense that they seemed provocative and necessary issues in the democratization debate. The first area was a consideration of equality of opportunity in education, particularly in terms of what innovative projects or progressive policies were trying to change and trying to achieve. The second was the question of the relationships between all the various individuals and groups who have an interest in schooling – teachers, pupils, parents and politicians. The third area was the issue of the relationship between educational practice and educational analysis; between action and research and between teachers and researchers. The final item, and arguably the most important, was the question of the pupils' influence on the processes of schooling; their influence on the learning process, on the organization and management of schools and classrooms and on the everyday routines and patterns of their lives in school. But these were just starting-points. In the chapters which follow, the issues are cut into and developed in many different ways.

In editing the chapters for the book, we have tried to accomplish two things. We have tried to preserve something of the spirit which flourished at the conference. It was a spirit of tolerance and warmth and was characterized by a great willingness to listen and to learn, to get into dialogue, despite differences of language, of culture and of personal persuasions. To this extent, in preparing the papers for an English readership, we have tried to retain something of the style or the voice of the original writers. It was also a spirit in which differences in status seemed irrelevant. And to this extent, we have mixed together contributions from different countries and from people holding different positions in the world of education.

There is a kind of logic to the order of the chapters in this book – although it is not crucial. The first part of the book contains the stories of educational innovations, these we hope to provide illustrations of what might be possible in a democratization process. In the second part of the book, we have arranged discussions of reflections on the issues which arise from the kinds of projects described in Part One. Both parts of the book start with chapters which focus on local themes and proceed through to discussion which emphasizes more global topics; from the level of the personal, through the institutional, to the level of the system. But we would stress that, in a democratization debate, no level is more significant than another; quite the contrary, they are locked together.

Introduction: Towards democratic schooling

KNUD JENSEN AND STEPHEN WALKER

The democratization of education is a process, a struggle, a moving and constantly shifting series of actions and desires. This makes the writing of this introduction difficult because even the reports and discussions collected in this book refer to projects and to ideas that are themselves in a state of flux. Some are finished, some are just developing, some are embryonic. What is reported and discussed in this book, then, is a series of how different teachers and educational researchers in various schools in Europe have attempted to change educational practices and thinking.

Each project has its own focus. Each discussion is based upon certain quite specific concerns. But in some way or other, all the papers in this collection address the question of how to move a step further along the path towards increasing the degree of democracy experienced in schools and classrooms.

So what is the movement? What is democratization? Almost impossible questions to answer. As the descriptions and debates which follow certainly illustrate, there is no common definition or agreed core concept. But there are certain stances which are to be adopted again and again in each discussion, certain assumptions which are constantly challenged. This suggests that whilst we cannot and do not claim that this book provides easy answers on the central goals and crucial strategies of a democratization movement, there are some basic themes which have to be confronted.

First, what view do we have of the child? Not the pupil, not the learner, but the child. Straightforward though this question might be, an explicit or implicit vision of the child shines through the different projects and programmes reported and analysed. This vision blends optimism and respect with responsibility and obligation. Children are not adults nor are they to be treated as such. But they are always to be seen as people who have an ever-growing capability to deal with new situations and as persons with whom one can negotiate and reach agreements.

This vision is not just a picture, a mental construct. For the writers in this book it becomes the basis for relationships, especially in the classroom or the school. If we are to keep faith with this image, if we are to act upon this perception, then it follows that adult–child relations will have to be shaped in a way which gives children the space to make choices and decisions, to extend their capacity for action and to honour any agreements into which they enter. To describe democratization in this way makes the process sound very simple. Obviously, a second basic question which one has to face is to do with how to initiate the kind of changes envisaged.

It is one thing to assert that one might like to create new spaces in the classroom for children but another thing to put this into practice. Where does the democratization process begin? With staff relations, with curriculum change, with teaching methods, with the internal organization of the school? Again, there is no single answer. However, the chapters in this book do indicate that the process of initiation might have certain common features. Certainly, none of the projects start with abstract discussions of democratic aims, goals and objectives. In each case, the process seems to have begun as a response to certain 'local' difficulties, to certain problems which arise directly from the real-life experiences of those involved. The precise catalyst for change might be any anxiety or concern: the educational performance of certain pupils, the desire to react to legislation or, maybe, teachers worrying about their working conditions. The exact starting place cannot be determined in advance: indeed, it would be contradictory to imagine that this was the case. Democratic change has to begin precisely where those involved feel there is a need. It is their choice.

But if the issue is choice, how are the differences which will inevitably arise from conflicts of interests or from competing perspectives to be managed? In this book, this particular theme is approached in two ways. First, a basic assumption to be found in many of the action or the experimental programmes is that differences of opinion, outlook, or interest are to be celebrated and cherished rather than hidden and repressed. It is assumed that children will have different opinions from adults on what is worth learning and what approaches are most useful; it is assumed that children from different cultural communities will have different understandings and different priorities; it is assumed that one group of teachers will champion one objective in the school which conflicts with that of another group. However, rather than see these as hurdles or deficiencies, the position taken in democratization projects is to regard them as challenges. The issue then becomes a question of how the school can respond and react to conflict and differences in a way which allows for equality of expression and conviction.

Recognizing differences in itself helps meet this challenge. If differences of opinion or perception can be defined as normal and healthy then this can surely provide a basis on which the partners to any project can gradually negotiate certain ways and means of coping with their competing claims. Certainly, we cannot imagine schools or classrooms where differences disappear, where everyone agrees basic procedures and priorities. But there is evidence in this book that although differences can never be dissolved, it is possible for different factions or interest groups or different groups of individuals to negotiate the basis on which conflicts can be managed. Reaching 'contracts' in this way means that not only are differences made more public but also that ways of coping with conflicts are collectively established.

Recognizing and respecting differences of interest and ambition is the *subject* of a democratization process. The *object* of the process is power-sharing. And this is really the pivot for the whole debate in this book – the fundamental and most difficult issue. Predictably, most projects come to this crucial concern through a consideration of how schools are implicated in the reproduction of social inequalities or are directly responsible for creating educational inequalities of experience and treatment. The actual expressions of inequality which have provoked the innovations and experiments in the projects are many. Each project centres on its own evaluation of which aspect of inequality is most vexatious. Inequality based on age differentiation in the adult–child or teacher–pupil relationships; inequality based on how schooling responds to cultural, class, or community differences; inequality based on ethnic or gender differentiation; and inequalities which spring from the ideological manipulation of the less powerful by those who wield power.

This variation in interest is important. As we have already observed, the struggle to initiate democratization processes in schools *has* to be located in experience of inequality or undemocratic routines, otherwise it has no meaning for those who are supposed to benefit, for the participants. But the variation of interest has another significance.

Basing innovation on an attack on inequality means that the issue of power-sharing is approached in an interesting way. First, because inequalities arise mainly from differences – cultural, positional, or economic – the emergent view of power-sharing is decidedly not reductionist. Democratic movements are often caricatured as attempts to obliterate power differences or to construct new power structures. This is not the view evidenced here.

The emergent vision of power-sharing is not one in which everyone is somehow reduced to the same levels of opportunity or perception, to a grey uniformity. We can never be equal in that sense. Rather, the view is one of trying to build opportunities whereby people with different needs and different skills have an equal chance to express their individuality and to take part in the negotiation of collectively agreed plans. Second, this view implies a basic analysis of power relationships as being a dialectical interaction between what Matheson (1987) has called power-holders and power-subjects – neither being independent of the other. In a democratization process, then, or at least on the evidence of the experiments in this book, a key concern becomes how to facilitate the ways in which power-holders and power-subjects negotiate. Or, to put it another way, discussions about equality become discussion about diversity.

To summarize. This book is not a series of prescriptions, a manual for political or education reform. It is a set of stories; stories about how certain people tried to change certain bits of daily life in schools and classrooms and stories about how people have thought about their experiences of these places. What the separate and idiosyncratic stories show, however, are certain similar visions – visions which, amazingly, have been nurtured by people working in different contexts, with different cultures and on different conditions. These visions give a glimpse of what the democratization of schooling minimally involves. It involves a view of the child as not yet self-reliant but with an essential capability of reaching a state of being able to think and to act independently. It involves a view of adults and of teachers as being responsible people, with a chance of making their own lives better by struggling to guide children in the direction of understanding the importance of other children's, other adults', rights to be different. It involves concentrating on the here and the now of social experience and not on some dream of a mysterious future. It involves disagreements and deals and making choices which will not always, which will not ever satisfy the ambitions of every individual. And it involves dialogue. It involves real people in passionate and personal debate – debate which is not about what they might do but about what they will do, together.

This vision, this view of what will be the basis for action in schools also entails a view of what will be an appropriate approach to analysis of such actions and experiences. In the second part of the book, 'The Debates', is a second set of stories, a collection of narratives about ways of researching and reflecting on educational issues and events in a manner which is broadly in line with the assumptions which have developed in the experimental projects. Again, there are no rules or predetermined procedures. But there are basic analytical stances. A stance towards blurring the status boundaries between theory and practice, between analysis and action. A stance towards systematically directing research into the problems and the ambitions of people who live in the world being investigated. A stance towards trying to combine systematic examination with personal attitudes, feelings and emotions. Essentially, a stance towards building a research style which is participatory and which consciously strives to encapsulate diversity, or the management of different aims, personal resources and anticipated outcomes. The division we use in this book, between experiments and debates, is a false one. There is no real division – only different kinds of stories, different people giving their version of what they found and what they thought. And we do not know how these stories will end, we can only speculate. We do not expect that every reader will agree with every strategy and every stance. But the writers of the narratives are trying to deal with the problems of inequality and diversity as they meet them. You may disagree with their questions and their responses but you will not find anything in the material which would allow you to conclude that they did not care. And that's what the stories are about.

Reference

Matheson, C. (1987). 'Weber and the classification of forms of legitimacy', *British Journal of Sociology*, vol. 32 (2).

PART 1

The experiments

CHAPTER 1

Participation and partnerships

The school at Iceland Wharf

Carl Bagge, Elisabeth Spaet Henriksen,
Svend Hesselholdt, Knud Jensen,
Ole B. Larsen and Hanne Schneider

Participation – The story of the school at Iceland Wharf

In the beginning there was a school – the school at Iceland Wharf.
But the school has special characteristics. It is situated in a well-
demarcated part of Copenhagen – only a few hundred metres from
the centre of the city.

For many years, the inhabitants of Iceland Wharf have worked to
establish the identity of the neighbourhood as a community and, as
part of this struggle, to build a completely developed school. The
community was established as a working-class quarter during the
years 1900 to 1920. Today the inhabitants are families who have
lived on the old wharf for several generations and others, mainly
students and 'guest workers', who have moved into the quarter
fairly recently.

What prompted the project which is reported in this chapter, were
some questions the teachers at the school began to worry about. Are
we really practising what we preach, what we believe? Are we giving
our pupils, as the Primary Education Act (1975) of Denmark stipulates, the rights to gain universal experience and to democratic joint
participation in school development? Are we listening to our

children and acting on what we hear? To help explore these questions, the teachers called for the assistance of educational researchers at the Royal Danish School of Education Studies (RDSES) – and the project began.

The researchers, working on the basis of their own research principles developed at the Laboratory of Democratic Educational Research, initiated an action-research programme with the teachers which concentrated on two concerns. How to identify issues and how to address them. Joint study groups were set up in the school and a period of joint consultation began, which lasted for the three years between 1983 and 1986.

The teacher–researcher study groups selected two areas as their main concern – the relationships between teachers in the organization of the school and relationships between teachers and pupils in the classroom. And then they started to investigate and to experiment. The story of this project begins with the view of the head-teacher.

The headteacher's tale

Carl Bagge

Half a year ago, one of our teachers was not at school. I went into the classroom and told the children what I imagined they were going to do for the day. So I told the children: 'Do so and so'.

Then some of the children arose from their chairs and said to me: 'Oh no, man – look here. We agreed with Hanne [the teacher] that we were going to work with this today. It was our own decision. Why have you changed that?'

And they pointed to what was written on the flip-chart.

This little story illustrates the use of the flip-chart, which is one of the main tools we use when we are working together with our students. It suggests that these tools with which we work, and have been working with for some years, seem to be having some effect on the children.

Before we started working together with the research team from RDSES, we had agreed that we were 'the teachers' too much: that we listened too little to the claims and aims of the children. We did not know what to do about it, so we asked the researchers for help. When the researchers came to our school, they did put their finger on two main sore points:

Firstly: Does democracy exist amongst the teachers?

Secondly: Does democracy exist amongst the children?

And so they organized the study groups, which worked for three or four years. What have the results been, now the scientists have left us? What is our school like today? Are there any traces left of what the study groups tried to do? I will try to illustrate the frames around democracy we created and explain what they allowed to be done.

In defining our school we found that very often the structure, the concepts, the contents and the methods used are mutual and dependent factors. We believe that it will be very difficult to develop a school if at the same time you do not develop both the contents of the school programme and the structure.

We formed this idea on the basis of our experiences and through discussions. We have had the possibility of these discussions in the teachers' group throughout the 16 years during which the school has existed. Each week the teachers have had a conference. For 16 years none of the teachers have been away from these conferences unless they were ill, and they have been present voluntarily. During our work with the researchers from the Royal Danish School of Educational Studies (RDSES), we tried to develop these conferences and make them better. We are following those guidelines today.

If you participated in our conferences for one month, you would see the following:

- In the first week we work with common, practical aims in the school.
- In the second week we discuss pedagogical questions, which might not have anything to do with our teaching of the moment. But it could also be planning a common topic, which we are going to develop in school.
- To make our conferences better we also decided to issue a newsletter for each conference. Furthermore, we decided that all the teachers in turn should be in the chair and, at another time, reporter – and, a third time, one will look after the coffee, which is important too.

To understand the work in the school, you need to know how big the school is. There are 25 teachers and others involved in education and 280 children. The school is organized around two big rooms. It is very tightly packed, we have very little space for each child. But that does not appear to influence the children and the teachers in a bad way. In some ways it is easier to work together more closely, because we will often find colleagues next door or in the big room between the classrooms.

The school's surroundings are very nice. The school is situated in the very centre of Copenhagen. But in spite of this, there is a park close to the school. We often receive visits from a fox and a nightingale in the schoolyard. So we are close to nature and we are close to civilization too.

What does this lead to? You are close to your school environment. You are able to use organizations, shops, and the community centre in the area as well. We would like the school, in the mind of the child, to be an entire world – not an atomized world, separate from the community. But, to achieve this, in the school itself, we therefore try to organize teaching in such a way that a child will have – and see – the world around him/her in a more entire way as well. But how is this done?

1. In our opinion it is important that only a few teachers work with a particular class. In some countries this is already a tradition, but in our country it is not.
2. Furthermore, we try to combine the resources an individual teacher has with resources we get from the central authority – so that we are able to have *two* teachers for most lessons. And lessons are designed to follow each other – module by module.
3. Last but not least:
   Children are not changing from topic to topic or from subject to subject. The children have time for what they are working at, to develop a topic to the fullest extent.

   As a consequence of this principle, we prefer the special training of children who might be backward readers etc. to be done in the classroom, and class teachers to be responsible themselves for teaching of children with special needs.

Within those frames we find it important that we teach the children *topics*. When teaching topics, a question is raised:

'When teaching *topics*, do you then abandon *subjects*?'

We have a saying in school, '*if you are teaching topics you need the subjects as tools*'.

Then it becomes interesting:

How do you now manage to do this together with the children?

I shall try to give an illustration by mentioning what we did in August 1987.

We decided at our teachers' meeting that for this year each class, as usual, would make their own *year-plan*, saying which topics we were going to study during the year.

At the teachers' meeting it was decided that we would like to find two topics among all the children's topics, which could be taught in common in the whole school. This is important in the school because teachers not only need to share experiences with their classes, but to share experiences with their colleagues. So how did this plan develop?

Before we answer this question, it is necessary to explain the pedagogical principles which we try to apply when we formulate topic work in the school and which we used as a basis for developing this particular plan in 1987.

The pedagogy

Ole B. Larsen and Knud Jensen

We adults and children experience things in different ways. Also, we have different attitudes, abilities and ways of reasoning. These differences create both barriers and opportunities for work in school. If we are to seize the chance to put these differences to good use in the school, we need to recognize that although we adults and children will differ in how we approach school work, this work has certain characteristics which do *not* vary and which are part of the essential nature of these activities. School work, like any other human activity can be divided into three component parts:

1. the forming of conceptions,
2. the taking of actions, and,
3. the evaluation of the results of the activities.

This process applies to whatever the activity and whoever is the agent.

Clearly, children can shape their own ideas about work in school and this is true of both the form and the content of this work. And their ideas can be used as a guideline in the development of school work. Obviously, not all ideas are realized from the start and not all actions take place smoothly. Similarly, conversation and co-operation with others is necessary for the actual execution of the whole activity and not all evaluations, therefore, can wait until the end. But if we are to help children to utilize *their* ideas and experiences in school work which is democratized, then we will need to make sure that they participate in each stage of the work process – conception, action and evaluation.

So what pedagogical principles might we apply so as to achieve such a goal?

Direct experience – workshop education

An education which seeks to give children democratic rights and co-influence must ensure that it is possible for them to gain direct experience. Workshop education must be arranged in such a way that the pupils gradually learn to manage the *whole* work process. It is important that experimentation is permitted and that the pupils see and experience some consequences of that work on which they themselves had influence.

As a way of anticipating the practical problems and possibilities of workshop education, we have distinguished six concepts which we normally see as three *pairs* of concepts, each pair being a personal and group association.

Freedom of speech and of opinion

The Danish Education Act lays down that pupils have the right to express themselves on issues to do with school work. But freedom of expression and public opinion belong together. There is nothing to gain from expressing oneself, if others do not listen, adopt an attitude and put forward their own proposals or comments. This is why we work with the concepts as a pair – the one side is the individual, the other side is the group.

Resourcefulness and self-administration

Resourcefulness concerns the individual's ability to take action. Self-administration is taking common responsibility for the fulfilment of agreements which have been entered into and also for the conditions which apply. Individuals must themselves, and in association with others, learn to administer as large a part of their lives as possible, and do this with solidarity. Resourcefulness and self-administration show themselves particularly when ideas and decisions need to be put into practice. This requires both skill and knowledge. Democratic ability is something other and above mere 'meeting techniques'.

Individual and collective development

The third pair of concepts is individual and collective development. A fellowship is built on interest, willingness, and agreements. The school is not a voluntary fellowship, and is based on a power structure. A restricted individual influence will often result in some of the pupils dominating the mutual relationship. The amplitude and fruitfulness of a fellowship are developed when its members have a free hand in developing themselves, and it is essential that the individual is able to visualize different possibilities of development for both the person and the collective.

Four fields of learning experiences

Workshop education must, therefore, provide the child with the possibility of gaining many different kinds of experience, and thereby of developing versatility. The model on which we work contains four fields of learning.

1. The child learns and gains experience when working manually in the production of something. We call this the manual–productive field.
2. The child learns and gains experience when experimenting and seeking knowledge in a systematic manner. We call this the scientific–experimental field.
3. The child learns and gains experience when active in an artistic and bodily way. We call this the artistic–bodily field.
4. A fourth kind of experience is gained by communicating and working together with others. The main emphasis here is placed on being active in discussion, in reading or writing. We call this the linguistic–social field.

Although in many cases the four fields overlap with each other, there are many ways in which they are different.

1. The manual–productive field

The characteristic aspect of the manual–productive field is that one produces something which one has conceived before starting the work. We talk about a democratically designed workshop education when the participants take an active part in the *concept* phase as well as in production and in outcome.

2. The scientific–experimental field

In the scientific–experimental field one does not always have a clear idea with regard to results, but some methods of approach and some provisional assumptions concerning what is likely to evolve are essential.

3. The artistic–bodily field

In the artistic–bodily field it is the sensuous aspect which is central for the perception and the forming of experience. When working with self-expression, it often proves that conception, production and evaluation succeed each other along the way. When judged to be good enough by those involved, the concept and the product phases fuse together.

4. The linguistic–social field

Although the linguistic–social activities arise in the other fields, we have chosen to retain this as a special field of experience. Activity in this field can thus be both the means for other fields and a subject in itself. Language is interaction and thus also a part of a social relationship. A considerable part of our cultural mediation is linguistic – in planning, in conversation, in song and in working with texts or with texts and pictures.

Cultural mediation

Cultural mediation is an essential part of the school's democratization, the reason being that an individual's concepts and expressions form part of mutual opinion, and they are the background for the understanding of differences and of our various conditions of life. The fundamental abilities in this field – of reading, writing and self-expression – are important in the development of one's own resourcefulness.

Several types of activities

To achieve the principles described above, our teachers prepare themselves in ways which are different from when preparing an ordinary class lesson. The preparation includes the following considerations:

- that there can be several types of activity in progress at the same time;
- that work is planned together with the children;
- that the possibilities of action are often open, and that there are many of them;
- that the phases in the work are made clear so that the process can be evaluated;
- that agreements are reached and maintained or changed.

A teacher's story

Hanne Schneider

This is a description of a course of education carried out in February 1986 in the school at Iceland Wharf. It will start with a short introduction of the class and continue with a description of topic-oriented instruction. Then follows the story about the topic: 'China and Japan'.

The class

At the time of the project the class consisted of 24 pupils and they had two teachers for almost all subjects and lessons. Since we also covered special education there were times when we were both with the class, while during other lessons we were alone with the class.

From the start of school, the class had been accustomed to being fairly big (28 in the first class), and to having two teachers to instruct them. Instruction had been topic-oriented, of a workshop nature, and greatly inspired by the RBS method – reading on the basis of speech. This is a reading–teaching method with phases during which:

1. the children's common experiences are worked out in a classroom discussion;

2. the main points are picked up for a very short story or description of the events;
3. the story is built up on the blackboard;
4. the text is re-read and possibly copied; and,
5. an analysis is made of the linguistic and grammatical features of the text.

At this particular time – February 1986 – we had just had some student teachers in the classroom, it had been a somewhat unsettled and confusing period for everyone. Both the pupils and teachers were in need of a long and settled period during which the work would ideally be with a well-considered and motivating subject.

What is workshop-organized core curriculum?

As an introduction to this new subject, the teachers decided that the class and the teachers together should try to define:

'What is a good topic?' and 'How does one work with a topic?'

The teachers decided to do this because, in connection with earlier subjects, there had often been different ideas about what constituted a topic and what topic work was. We had often experienced that the topics proposed by the pupils were very 'narrow' – almost in the form of a question that could be answered by a 'yes' or a 'no' – and consequently the teachers had found themselves having to put some 'meat' on the subject. As teachers we thought that the pupils should now be better able to consider the choice of topic, and to find out what a given topic had to offer in the way of content, working methods and aims. This was not only in order that the new topic should be given some careful consideration, but also with a view to planning future work.

Choice of topic

We asked the children in the class for their definitions of a 'topic', and after a class discussion we wrote the following up on our flip-chart:

1. When one works with topics, one learns something.
2. When working with topics, one is studious.
3. When working with topics, the class works together.
4. When working with topics, one makes presentations (i.e. a group of pupils describe and show, and possibly dramatize what they have made in their group) so that the other pupils can learn

something from them. At the same time, the other pupils and the teachers evaluate the group's work.

5. When one works with a topic, one gets to know something.
6. When working with topics, one receives answers to one's questions.

To the question of *how* one works with topics, the children answered:

1. by seeing films,
2. by reading,
3. by being outside the school,
4. by visiting museums,
5. by making something with one's own hands,
6. by writing,
7. by talking,
8. by putting on plays,
9. by singing,
10. by dancing,
11. by carrying out experiments,
12. by drawing.

It can be seen from the above, that there is good balance between the pupils' concepts of how one works with topics, and that which the teachers call the four fields. The fields involved here are the following experience fields, described in the previous section of this chapter:

1. The manual–productive field.
2. The artistic–bodily field.
3. The scientific–experimental field.
4. The linguistic–social field.

We have found it to be a good idea for teachers to make use of this model in order to ensure that pupils gain all-round experience.

We have now reached the point where that class and the teachers in co-operation decide what the coming topic should be.

Conception phase

All of the children are provided with a piece of paper on which they are required to write their proposals for the next topic. The pieces of paper ensure that they all consider the matter, write something down and participate in the process. When they have all been given enough time, all of the pupils' suggestions are written up on the blackboard. Some of them are amplified by the relevant pupil, other pupils, or the teachers. Some of the suggestions are discarded if they do not conform with our common idea of what topic work is about.

On this occasion, the topics were animals, horses, birds, circus, undeveloped countries, the handicapped, food, sweets, flowers, China, Japan, Hong Kong, Greenland, the USA, shipping, transport, films, war and peace.

The topics are categorized on the board, discussed and examined. Many pupils abandon their own suggestions, because they think that other suggestions are better. After a while, we take a vote and our new topic is to be 'China and Japan'.

We now enter into what we call the conception phase. We want to know what the pupils know beforehand, and what expectations they have with regard to how the topic will progress. This time, the pupils form pairs and use a computer text-processing facility to write down what they know or imagine about the topic: 'China and Japan'. These concepts are stored on discs, after having been studied by the teachers.

From a reading of the pupils' ideas, the teachers find it necessary to give them some concrete information of a geographical and historical kind concerning China and Japan. Therefore, with the aid of an atlas and films, the teachers provide a brief survey of some important geographical and historical facts concerning the two countries.

Action phase

The children were then asked: 'How and where can we get to know something more about China and Japan?'

All the children write their answers on a piece of paper, and all of the answers are collected on our flip-chart. This ensures that they all participate in the process, and in this way they become responsible for the future work.

The children answer the question with:

We can get to know something by
1. reading,
2. seeing films and slides,
3. by seeing exhibitions and visiting museums,
4. by asking someone who has been there,
5. using the telephone to ask someone,

6. asking someone in a steak-house,
7. making enquiries at travel bureaux,
8. asking at the embassies,
9. asking the press – reading newspapers,
10. talking with friendship societies.

It proved that two of the pupils had family members who could help us.

In order to get started on the work, we collected all the books we could find in the school library and from the school library's common collection, including picture-books.

Back in the classroom, each child selected a book which they were required to read and to provide a report and review of a couple of days later. In order to control who had which book, we wrote it up on the flip-chart, and when the book was referred to by the pupil. We also wrote down some cues so that everybody gradually formed a picture of what the individual books could be used for. A single, very weak reader took a picture-book home which his mother read aloud for him. The next day he gave an excellent account of the book on the basis of the pictures, and was thus fully able to participate in the work of reviewing the books.

In our workshop technique, on the basis of what the pupils now know concerning the topic, a series of subtopics emerge, and the children choose what they want to examine more closely. This results in the next phase, which is group work. The pupils suggest part-topics and these are written up on the flip-chart. The part-topics for this project were: (1) Agriculture, (2) War, (3) Animals, (4) Religion, (5) The Old China, (6) The New China, (7) Tokyo, (8) Inventions.

The pupils write down on a piece of paper those themes in which they are particularly interested. The teachers then form subgroups based on the wishes of the pupils, and also on the basis of the teachers' knowledge concerning the children's abilities to co-operate, and such that the groups formed are of a reasonable size.

In addition in reading and writing, the children in the groups worked with various workshop-oriented activities: the production of posters; the making of a doll's house arranged in the fashion of a Japanese house; the making of cut-out dolls, simple agricultural tools and maps; and the performance of a shadow play. (Along the way the children found out that many of their toys had been made in Hong Kong, Japan and China, and this resulted in an exhibition of toys being held in the class.)

The following joint activities were arranged for the whole class:

- We received a visit by someone who had been in China.
- He gave a lecture with the help of slides.
- We visited the China and Japan department of the National Museum.
- We were provided with the possibility of having some silk moth larvae in the class, and we were able to see how they developed.
- We had a visit from a Tai Chi teacher who demonstrated Tai Chi and explained it to us.

All of the texts which the pupils had written concerning their part-topics were collected and printed together with the texts which they had written at the start of the topic work.

Evaluation phase

The project suffered an abrupt end when the school, for reasons of renovation, had to move over to another building, and we could not take our materials with us. However, we made an evaluation during which we read aloud and put forward our criticisms, but since we did not have all our materials, a true evaluation was not possible. Otherwise the evaluation comprised of the individual groups explaining and showing the others what they had made. The other children and the teachers posed questions and put forward criticism.

Another form of evaluation is when the individual pupils write a story in which, for example, they imagine being a child in present-day China. These stories are then read aloud to the class for comments. At other times the teachers put forward questions which must be answered in writing by the pupils individually. The questions could be, for example:

1. Have you learned something that you did not know before?
2. Are you satisfied with the efforts you have made in your work?
3. Can you use what you have learned in other connections?
4. What would you like to work further with?

In the same manner, the teachers discuss between themselves how the topic work has progressed. What should be changed next time? What did we forget? What was especially good and bad?

And in these ways, we gave our pupils more control of both the content of the topics they studied and of methods they used and we hope they are able to see the phases of the work process which is the same for all school activities.

CHAPTER 2

Insiders and outsiders

REFLECTING ON THE ICELAND WHARF PROJECT

(i) Self-direction as a democratic feed-forward process

Svend Hesselholdt

Postulates

- In the democratization of education the teacher makes necessary knowledge visible to help children make their interests and ideas explicit.
- In democratic co-operation the domination of the strongest child is reduced when the group discuss all ideas using that knowledge the teacher has made visible.

Self-direction, then, can be seen as one important aspect of the democratization of a school. So one focus in the project 'The School at Iceland Wharf' was concerned with a single question: *How could self-direction be achieved practically in the project-oriented form of education characteristic of this school and described by Hanne Schneider, in Chapter 1?*

Concepts

Self-direction can be split up into two aspects:

- *Influence* on what might be the objectives and themes of any project, and,
- *'Self-steering'*, that is, acting on the basis of the decisions about objectives.

These two aspects must not be seen as unrelated. The researchers in this project have formulated three pairs of democratic principles, which can illustrate how they relate, and the concept of self-direction.

Each pair has an individual and a collective side. The first pair is 'freedom of speech' and the group's 'opinion'. Self-direction as *influence* is the individual's expression of his or her ideas about the project, but as project-work often is group work, the groups discuss the individual's ideas – they form an opinion.

Self-direction as *self-steering* is related to the second pair – resource-fulness and self-administration – because this pair is to do with the individuals' and the groups' realization of their decisions.

Thus self-direction is intimately related both to the individuals' and the collectives' development (the third pair).

The concept of self-direction has been used in much socialization research to do with upbringing at home (Kohn 1969; Hesselholdt and Kaad 1976). In that research the concept is often defined rather individualistically, as Holter (1975) has pointed out.

The concept of self-direction can also be understood in relation to the three-phase model we have used in the analysis of the phases in project-work and school activity.

In the '*conception phase*' the children formulate and discuss ideas about the project. In the '*action phase*' the individuals steer themselves and co-operate in realizing their initial ideas. And last, the teacher and the children evaluate both the group-process and the products. In this '*evaluation phase*' the group formulate themselves what could be called a '*feedback*'. But they also ask: How could we use what we have learned in the next project?

This activity could be called *feed-forward*. Feed-forward is often in the form of questions formulated in the conception phase on the basis of pre-knowledge questions which are answered in the action phase. The answers are evaluated in the evaluation phase and so on. This process is not only an individual activity. The ideas must be discussed with the other children, in the group and with the teacher. So the development of democracy in projects is the formation of *democratic feed-forward*.

Questions

(a) What is the role of the teacher?

The teacher has at least three very important roles:

1. Before the project starts she has given the children some relevant insight. For example, sometimes it is biological generalizations, sometimes it is structural components in story-telling.
2. At the start of the project she must give the help necessary for the choice of project-type.
3. She must help the children to bring their ideas into a form appropriate for project work.

   This very important task sometimes takes the form of helping pupils to formulate 'how to work' and sometimes it is help with formulating questions.

All these points are important for the future development of the project-oriented education, especially if it intends to be part of a democratic development. Examples can illustrate some of the problems the teacher and the children have to cope with.

1. Relevant knowledge before or in relation *to children's questions*
During project work, the children use some pre-knowledge. They have to learn how to word questions so that they are relevant for the work in question.

Soon after I saw the problems of self-steering emerge in the Iceland Wharf project, I was working with a senior lecturer in Biology; we teach (together) a course for teachers (in-service training). We found some systematic ways in which teachers can help children reformulate 'why questions' about biological problems. When the child's question is reformulated, she can formulate tentative 'hypotheses'. But, when the child formulates these hypotheses she must have access in her mind to some biological generalizations, which are relevant for the problems in question. The next step for the child is to understand, in a creative way, questions like: What are the consequences of my 'hypotheses'? Should I look in books? Should I make an experiment – and how might I design that experiment?

It is clear, then, that democratic education is much more than the simple question of 'Should we give the children influence or not?'

It is also a problem concerning issues like: How and when should the children be taught things like biological generalizations? And how should we teach the children experimental methodology? In answering these questions, it is essential to remember that what the children come to know they will use in a self-steering process; and the process will move from *their* questions to the *biologically relevant* answers to these questions. Thus the sequence is: Relevant pre-knowledge, conception phase, action phase, evaluation phase. And this sequence is repeated as each new project begins.

2. The teacher's second important role in the conception phase
Usually the teacher decides what kind of project is to be studied.
Therefore, the teacher must know and the children must learn that
there are at least three different kinds of project-activities:

 (i) Should we *study* these phenomena?
 (ii) Should we *judge* these phenomena?
(iii) Should we *change* the phenomena?

These three different types of project-activities lead to very different types of questions. In my experience, the first kind of activity
is infinitely more common than the second type; and the third kind is
very, very seldom raised.

All three kinds of activities give different kinds of influence to the
children. The first and domineering form has its roots in the child's
curiosity – to know more about the world and life in general. It is
different from that form of education where outside forces completely alienate the child from access to his/her own interests. But
influence in a democratic society should also be influence understood
as the ability and the will to change the world in accordance with
one's understanding of life qualities. To develop project-oriented
education, therefore, it is important to discuss: *What kind of action-
research could promote 'influence as change'?*

The teachers at Iceland Wharf had stated 10–20 fundamental
values which should be the basis of the education at the school. One
of the values was: 'Critical responsibility for the near and the remote
milieu' (Skolen på Islands Brygge 1985). Now, *at least this one of the
fundamental values can only have an effect in project-oriented education if
you design the project to bring about active change of the school district.*

But before you can have this kind of influence, you must have
some ideas about values. You and your students might ask: 'What is
good and what is not so good in our district?' In this project, when
faced with this issue, the study groups we had established identified
five groups of themes with which we wanted to work. One of these
themes was: 'In which way does the school use the school's district
and the people in it, in project-oriented education?'

At Iceland Wharf there have been a few projects of the last-
mentioned type. One project was about pollution in some little
ponds near the school. Another was a plan for the traffic near the
school. A last example was a project where one group visited a
baker's shop in the district. The baker told the children that the shop
would be closed in a month. This information was handed by me
to the next group, who were to visit the baker's shop. This

group became indignant and formulated much more critical questions about why the supermarket had to close this part of the business.

In recent years, there have been many arguments about making school more open to life outside. And many suggest that the school should co-operate in various ways with parents. Perhaps it is possible to make projects in the school district where teacher, children and parents work together to make changes. Co-operation of this kind would make new demands also to researchers engaged in the projects.

(b) How can teachers help children to formulate their own good questions? Or:

The long road from idea, through questions to books and answers.

In the conception phase of a project the children introduce some ideas to do with what it would be interesting to know more about. These ideas must be shaped into a plan for searching for information. This plan could be made concrete by formulating the ideas of interest as *questions*. The questions can guide the children's search for answers to their questions. This process has been called *feed-forward* and is illustrated in the following two stories.

A pilot project concerning self-direction

The teacher's intention for this project was to study if it was possible in one week to carry out a project in which the children studied a theme *and* learned something about: 'What is a good project?'

The children followed a procedure which they had used many times. They made a list of suggestions for the project. Most of the children made choices concerning sex and puberty. 'What happens to girls? And what happens to boys?' These questions guided one little group.

First, of course, to begin the topic, they got some relevant books and then the questions guided them in scanning through the books until they identified the relevant places in the text, and at last they read what they wanted to know.

Another group made little stories about emotions related to puberty and marriage. One group were working with questions of abortions at a very high level.

But one group wanted to work with cartoons or jokes. This group was inspired by a television programme. The group attended the two teachers' sex instruction lesson and the other groups' presentation of their results. But the group also worked with their own theme. The teachers wanted them to evaluate jokes and categories of jokes, instead of only telling jokes to each other. The reason was that just *telling* jokes was not seen as likely to produce new insights. In contrast to the other groups this group did not work very well and their results were reproductions of jokes and so on.

One conclusion of this project is that an important condition for a project to be a goal-directed process, which the children themselves are steering, is that before they start the project they must have at least a vague idea about how to work with the theme (see above). Furthermore, they would do well to formulate a 'question' which could help them to steer the work. For example, in this project, it might have been: 'What makes jokes good?'

The children could not find answers to such a difficult question and the teachers had too little time to find materials to help the group. So the group did not work very well.

In this special project the intentions were to learn about: 'What characterizes a good project?'

In the talk about the work of the groups, the 'joking-group' could learn something about this important democratic problem. One could even say: Because they did *not* get new insight about joking, they learned about project-work, especially what are the conditions for self-steering in projects. Perhaps they understood that it is necessary to formulate problems (questions) that could guide their work. I call this process *feed-forward* or, if it is in a classroom like this one, *democratic feed-forward* because the conception with which the children use to steer themselves is formulated in a dialogue between teacher and pupils, and in a co-operation between children in the group.

Perhaps they also understood that it is not enough to formulate guiding questions; it is important that there is a fair chance of finding answers (in spite of the importance of daring to take risks).

I have already stated that the teachers at the school had formulated some fundamental values, which they wanted to promote at the school. One of these values was: 'to develop a sense of humour and self-irony' (Skolen på Islands Brygge 1985).

Now, as the project described above is a difficult theme, it could have been made into a teacher-project, to address the question: 'How can we help children in this development?'

Sometimes children formulate projects in areas where the teacher has little knowledge or experience. And the question arises as to how these can be developed in a way which satisfies both curricula and children's interests. This is what the research team calls *the teachers' methodological flexibility*.

The concept points to the ability of the teacher to understand what the children are interested in and, at the same time, to try to make this interest relevant for something the children have not yet learned and which could be relevant for each child's progress in learning. In a series of projects the child, of course, should have a progression of insights. That is why each project must be finished with a reflection: 'What have we learned, and what shall we therefore learn next?'

A necessary condition for democratic co-operation

In the project at Iceland Wharf, the researchers have mostly been in contact with the teachers, and that alone took much time and energy. Our interpretations are often built on the teachers' reports of what happens. The next example is based on children's products: four free texts.

A project about creation of a free text

The teachers in one 4th grade class wanted to have the children use computers, to which they had a limited access. They formed four groups with five or six children in each group. Their task was to write a fairy tale. But as there could only be two children in front of the computer at a time, they wrote it in this way: At first two children did some writing, then two others took over, and, eventually, two other children finished the story.

The research team had pointed out on many occasions that it is important to start a project by building a concept about what is going to happen. If a group is to co-operate they must build some kind of common conception, in this case a common outline of the fairy tale.

It is interesting to see what happened in this project because the children did not start by entering into a discussion about the outline of the story: three of the four stories were, therefore, not coherent.

In one group, two girls start writing a story about a girl who runs away from an orphanage. She comes into a cave where she sees a golden light. As the title is 'The Goldstone', there is no doubt that their intention is that the light should come from this goldstone.

But now two boys take over the writing of the story, and they want the story to be a crime story. This intention is seen in their sudden introduction of five or more very expensive cars in the cave and two men who have a clear resemblance to a negative superman. These two men try in vain to catch the girl, but fortunately she escapes with a bagful of diamonds.

But the two other children take over the writing and bring back the goldstone theme.

Co-operation between children is an important part of development of democracy in school. Seen in relation to the theme in this paper, 'self-direction', the example illustrates the importance of building a kind of 'feed-forward process' which is essential for democratic co-operation.

But what the *basis* of the common concept could be is a serious problem. There are some indications in the stories that the basis could be the theme, which could be expressed in the title. It could also be various structural elements characteristic of fairy tales.

It is essential for the self-steering person to know and to be able to use structural components. In the steering of yourself, when you write a story, you must make a sequence of choices. One choice is: 'What does the hero need?' Another choice is: 'Should the hero be tested in some way?'

The same structural components are important for a group of pupils writing a story together. The members of the group must discuss: Should the hero be tested in the story or should he not be tested? If they cannot reach an agreement they have to write two stories.

It is possible for the teacher to tell the children about the structural elements in fairy tales, and thereby help the children to discuss what their text should be about. To tell a fairy tale is a rather free project, but this does not mean that the teacher sits in a corner doing nothing. The democratic teacher is an active person.

References

Hesselholdt, S. and Kaad, U. (1976). '113 danske familiers bidrag til en belysning, af de socialt betingede opdragelsesforskelle, in J. Gregersen and O. Varming (eds.), *Paedogogisk psykologi, undervisningspsykologi.* Copenhagen, Arnold Busk.

Holter, H. (ed.) (1975). *Familien i klassesamfundet.* Oslo, Pax.

Kohn, M. (1969). *Class and Conformity. A study in Values.* Homewood, Ill., The Dorsey Press.

Skolen på Islands Brygge (1985). *Saadan? Hvad nu?* Copenhagen, Royal Danish School of Educational Studies (RDSES), Pedagogy and Psychology Papers 30.

(ii) School-logic as a barrier in teaching

Elisabeth Spaet Henriksen

At the start of the Iceland Wharf project, I was convinced that, in the first few years of schooling, there would be enough scope – particularly – to create learning processes which increased the pupils' influence on the contents of education, on the learning process and on the school's everyday activity. Obviously, this would have to mean that pupils have a better chance of being heard and, better still, of being taken seriously. Thus, my main interest in the project is the emancipation of pupils and an evaluation of teachers as a tool in this process (Henriksen *et al.* 1984 and 1986; Jensen *et al.* 1988).

One aspect of emancipation of children and pupils is that they are allowed to develop their own understanding of which abilities it might be useful to develop in oneself. Too often, teachers unconsciously interpret the children's ideas and proposals for work into their own conception of what is useful. These habits and rituals are often referred to as the logic of the institution, and in school, we might call it *school-logic*. (The concept is related to Bourdieu's notion of '*Habitues*'.)

There has been a tendency to ascribe this logic directly to the institution – as if the logic was *in* the institution and incorporated in certain parts of the structure. But I think that, in fact, this logic is not *in* the institution but, rather, in the ways in which schooling is perceived and comprehended. If this is the case, when we aim to transfer educational practice it will be important to be conscious of what people recognize as habits and rituals and how and to what extent these views and these practices are barriers to change.

As I talked to teachers and pupils at Iceland Wharf and as I observed them in the classroom, I noticed a difference between how people *talked* about changes in routines or praxis (usually in terms of smooth transition) and the reality of change. In reality, when teachers described change, their responses could be categorized in three levels:

1. Pure lip-service. (Find out what the researcher wants and describe the phenomena in their vocabulary.)
2. Confident assertion. (Confident claims that routines or praxis has really changed. Closer analysis reveals that there has been no

change in the essential process – the way of letting pupils influence the learning process. This means that there is no real change of basic habits.)
3. Real change. (Change has occurred to the extent that teachers use their didactic understanding to display what has happened – in terms, say, of pupils' influence or the teaching methods they *now* use to increase this influence. If this happens, it will be available in the teachers' description of their rituals, routines and habits; they will emphasize as important other traits than those they used before.)

As I developed these categories, I began to see the initial impact that the action-research project was having upon the teachers with whom we were working.

At first, the teacher obtains a much more varied understanding of the learning process in relation to a democratic perspective with emphasis on the children's influence. You can hear that they talk in another way about reality and they use the vocabulary in their teaching. In other words, the researchers have succeeded in having taught the teachers some of their theories. But has reality really changed? Do the children really act in a way other than before, or, if they do, is it then on matters that really concern them, or have they changed only because the teachers have been inspired to propose some new ideas?

In educational development projects dealing with equality, equal work and the right for children to have influence on their own learning process, it is not sufficient to develop common concepts of theory, but the aim is to change the daily routines of school life. But, by analysing my data I began to see that it was very difficult for the teachers to overcome some barriers, some old habits formed over a long, long time in the school. It is my view that institutions, including schools, are dominated by habits and rituals that work as barriers to innovation. New theories, new insight and understanding have a tendency to be adjusted to fit to the usual style. And the usual style in schools is that you don't take the children's proposals seriously. When the main point is that pupils should have influence on the contents of the learning process, which includes influence on decisions concerning what is important to learn, then it would be a barrier if teachers work with the prejudice that pupils don't understand much.

The school curriculum provides guidance on what to learn. But it is the teachers' understanding of democracy, their perception of what knowledge is and their insight into teaching methods that will determine how children's contributions are used.

It is, then, the reflexive consciousness of individuals which determines the way individuals meet with institutions. According to Berger and Lukmann (1966), if you intend to let pupils' influence on the learning process be used as a serious didactic principle, you have to demolish that logic which implies that the grown-ups possess all the knowledge and the children none. You may, according to Berger and Luckmann (1966), define knowledge as the total sum of what all men know about social reality. Knowledge at this level is a collection of maxims, morals, 'proverbs', 'pearls of wisdom', values, myths and so on. This knowledge is the greatest and most important in society. It is knowledge at this level which children – and grown-up people too – possess, when they start a learning process in a new subject.

The teacher possesses theoretical knowledge concerning the subject, but she will often fail to see that the children have a practical pre-knowledge which is quite valuable as theoretical knowledge. The problem is, how can you develop a way of teaching which can help the children to transform non-theoretical knowledge into theoretical knowledge, so that the pupils experience that they can *use* what they learn – in both present and future projects.

The didactic stretegies that we and the teachers at Iceland Wharf developed together, can be used as tools in this democratic learning process. The following example may illustrate the point.

In the beginning of a subject called 'Children in foreign countries' the teachers made a list of what were the most important things to learn something about. Then they asked the children what they thought it was important to know. The teachers were very surprised when they found that the children's proposals included nearly all of the things that the teachers themselves had proposed.

But they also proposed some new things to which the teachers had not given any thought whatsoever. For instance: 'How can it be that a father in Tanzania manages to have two wives?' The question, with a basis in non-theoretical knowledge, was used as a start for working with knowledge from the area of ethnography. The teacher had to develop her own theoretical knowledge about this subject. But the case has a little postscript:

When the work with Tanzania was over, the teacher asked the boy who had posed the question if he thought he had received an answer. The boy answered: 'Yes'. But when the teacher asked him why he had posed this particular question, he said that the reason was that *his* father could not manage two wives!

So, in a sense, the barriers were not quite surmounted: The teacher was only able to use the child's question as an impulse to widen her own meaning of what knowledge was, here, for example, to use an ethnographic point of view.

The teacher's conception about what knowledge was appropriate – that it was a psychological/sociological problem that primarily engaged the boy – was a barrier to be surmounted. If the teacher had discovered what sort of knowledge the boy's question was seeking, she would perhaps not have felt competent to make use of this in the learning process, or she may have considered it as being irrelevant. In my opinion, the greatest difficulties exist in how you manage to advance the pupils' influence on the content of education, and at the same time succeed in working with 'qualified' subject matter: 'qualified' both in relation to what is useful for the pupils now and later, and in relation to a broad comprehension of what theoretical knowledge may include.

We may put these questions: 'Are all concepts relevant and useful in teaching?'

'Can knowledge include experiences from the private sphere?'

For me, these are essential questions when we work towards increasing pupils' influence on the learning process.

Another problem in connection with eliminating the barriers – the 'logics' – is that it appears that *insight* concerning the existence of barriers (and awareness of their substance) is not always enough to change praxis and to enable people to *act* in another way. I have earlier described three levels of changing praxis. But when you analyse our interviews with the teachers, they mention that perhaps their greatest problem is how to give up power and at the same time maintain the quality of learning. It is quite certain that the teachers did not succeed in eliminating the barriers, but then to have expected them to do so would have been very naive. However, I think some of them succeeded in minimizing them. The first step is to be aware of the barriers.

But one thing is clear: The teachers at Iceland Wharf now talk about reality in another way than they did before. And there are many signs to indicate that the teachers will (gradually) become aware that non-theoretical knowledge and theoretical knowledge are aspects of the same case.

References

Berger, P.L. and Luckmann, T. (1966). *The Social Construction of Reality*. Harmondsworth, Penguin.

Henriksen, E., Hesselholdt, S., Jensen, K. and Larsen, O. (1984). *Intervention og magt*. Copenhagen, Royal Danish School of Educational Studies, Pedagogy and Psychology Papers 30.

Henriksen, E., Hesselholdt, S., Jensen, K. and Larsen, O. (1986). *The Democratization of Education*. Copenhagen, Royal Danish School of Educational Studies.

Jensen, K. Henriksen, E., Hesselholdt, S. and Larsen, O. (1988). *Et foraars arbejde med demokratisering*. Copenhagen, Royal Danish School of Educational Studies, Pedagogy and Psychology Papers 39A.

(iii) School democratization – a question of goal-directed work on power and influence

Ole B. Larsen

The school – a democratic culture

During recent years, a central discussion of 'quality in education' has been raised in the USA and in the West European school systems. Part of the criticism levelled at schools in this discussion has been about how, in their emphasis on 'basic skills', schools have been too concerned with cultural transmission and with giving qualifications as a preparation for the world of work. In this section of our chapter, a central argument will be that experience and knowledge are the tools of autonomy, and work in school is not merely to transmit but to *produce* culture. This culture can be impressed by democratic or by totalitarian traits. So the question of quality in education has to be seen in the light of the everyday socialization of participants in an institution.

The approach – basic assumptions

The Iceland Wharf project needed policies and strategies of intervention, which could enlighten and deal with preparing goal-directed work on the power distribution in the school.

The preconditions were to some extent advantageous. The school concerned had requested support for a pedogogical development project in many areas, among others working out a multidisciplinary core curriculum, the reorganization of the structure of special support for problem children, and elaboration of team teaching for the staff. When our research laboratory approached this request for support, we had, to some extent, fixed the agenda to the following scheme:

Phase 1   *Analysing*: Establishing dialogue between researchers and the staff.

Phase 2   *Planning*: Elaborating and planning tools for mutual publicity and individual influence on the problems of the staff.

Phase 3   *Action*: Assisting and supporting pedagogical initiatives for changes in school policy and daily life.

The rationale for this schedule was based upon two basic assumptions:

1. The adult participants of the school needed to experience the problems of democratization as existential questions before moving it to the teaching–learning situation of the classroom.
2. In action-research on democratization it was contradictory to implant theoretical understandings about teacher behaviour and possible changes before they could be attached to themes already given high priority by the staff.

Researcher interventions

1. Establishing the dialogue

The results of other research had highlighted the high risk of traditional features in teamwork between theoreticians and experienced teachers. The risks include the tendency among high-status persons to take over at a very rapid rate, and on the basis of 'over-rational' reasons, the full responsibility of the total situation: that is, control of the content as well as the course of the dialogue. To avoid this suppressing interactional pattern, our preliminary work consisted of individual interviews (tape-recorded) with single members of the teaching staff, covering questions about the fortunes and fallacies of the school, relations with parents, and relations between staff. Two courses of initial action emerged from this:

1. to anonymize and return to the full staff what they had said, so as to make the 'experienced social reality' public to the staff, and,

2. to analyse the behaviour and the suppressing features in the researcher–teacher relations.

The result was alarming. Even these brilliant, democratic-minded researchers and teachers showed several talents for establishing guru–disciple-like attitudes. Some examples of guru–disciple behaviours will illustrate this trend:

GURU **persuasion/mystification**	**DISCIPLE** **submission**
To translate the utterances of teachers into one's own concepts and understanding – without questions	To give beautiful lip-service to the explanations of the master.
To set up closed sets of principles (holy laws) which exclusively determine the reference of a setting.	To ask for principles instead of expressing one's own experience and generalizations.
To control the course of meetings through arrogance and the appropriation of time with statements which are congruent to own ideas.	Expressing questions and letting the leader build up the conclusions. Keep back resistance and disagreement.
Side-stepping the topic/theme to a field where the interest and knowledge of the theorist resides, i.e. by introducing quite specific words as keys to the participant's self-understanding (except the guru).	Giving up the origin of the theme and permitting new factions of insight to come.

This analysis and the discussion which followed among the staff served as a self-critical platform, which showed some barriers to democratization, namely the unconscious demonstration of classical behaviour by high- and low-status persons when in dialogue.

This tendency towards academic guru–disciple behaviour was re-analysed much later in the project, and has shown some radical change. Perhaps the participants can be said to have relearned a more symmetric egalitarian behaviour between grown-up people. Such was the intention.

2. Conditions for teachers' planning

This project was also directed towards working on the circumstances and conditions of the teachers' working life. But, to keep
faith with our basic principle of publicity and freedom of expression,
we needed a basis for commonly acceptable development. A tool for
this was a questionnaire, which already existed, the material of the
project Nordstress. The teachers had their own answers returned to
them, in plenum, for studying and discussion. In such meetings, the
researcher group formed a special partnership, described elsewhere.
The point is that the researchers' roles become split into two: An
observer (the registrar) and one fully engaged participant (the facili-
tator) in the discussion. In this way we have the possibility of serving
the meetings with:

1. A secretary function and (over time) support to the memory of
    the group,
    and,
2. An initiating and encouraging function to enhance the dynamic
    aspect, the will to analyse and to invent changes in the group.

By making the two roles explicit and public we can counteract the
temptation to persuade the staff to premature changes based on
rhetoric alone. The observer will intervene as and when s/he is
conscious of suppressing trends of the meeting.

   The opportunity of sharing knowledge of the collegial working
situation of the staff (e.g. the sharing of privileges and duties) is to
make 'social reality' a little bit more transparent, and ideas of
blocking conditions can eventually be turned into proposals for new
deals. At least the differences of personal interests will be more
visible, and factions may be established.

   The agreement between the teachers and the researchers of anony-
mity causes special difficulties for the researcher to publish (outside
the staff) the results of this type of intervention, but we can state that
some working schedules were changed for the staff – and the levels of
mutual reasoning raised. Later the staff repeated this approach
without researcher assistance.

3. Teachers' mutual didactic conceptions

One of our basic assumptions was that questions of democratization
had some parallel characters in adult– and teacher–child relations.

   To this end we set up three pairs of concepts to illuminate the
crucial items of a democratic setting:

- Publicity and freedom of expression.
- Self-administration and resourcefulness.
- The collective's and the individual's development.

The cornerstone in pedagogical development here was in our concept of the teacher. Her fantasy and idea of legitimate actions form, to a very high degree, a framework for development in the daily life of school.

Therefore, the barriers and opportunities which staff themselves identified were useful starting points for problematizing and making proposals for change.

In three study-groups the teachers discussed the pedagogical policy with regard to:

1. The teaching–learning process – and children's admittance to influence through negotiations and mutual agreements.
2. Ways of opening up the concept of curriculum, by taking the interests and understanding of children seriously.
3. The relation between the school and the local environment – especially the channels and procedures of co-operation between school and parents.

The discussion of the three themes and the proposals for change can be found in a public report made out by the teacher group (Borg *et al.* 1981).

These themes cannot be discussed in detail here, but it was a recognizable result of this starting-point, that a many-faceted curricular understanding was much more eagerly introduced in the staff; perhaps this is why today, in a much more relaxed climate, they have worked out their own criteria for good education – and therefore see their disagreements and alliances in a clearer light.

The work of this school is today built upon the (almost) fully agreed conviction that the sooner children share in didactic questions of what and why to learn, the more human-like will be the results.

Therefore, the teachers try to share ideas, curriculum content, negotiations about working methods – and evaluation – with the children.

We don't say it always succeeds. But, they try their hardest.

Results – recent developments

Some changes have survived the end of the action-research project at Iceland Wharf. Greater publicity of teachers' shared working problems were established during the project period. The course of the staff meetings has changed. The great amount of information which is necessary in a modern school, is generally given in print, while the teachers' council determines the priority of items for dialogue and new deals.

Today, the problems of didactic changes are tackled through the school's self-monitored curricular project, for which the staff get financial support from the local educational authorities. The principle of opening the curriculum (i.e. making it more flexible in content and lesson organization) is maintained, and interest today focuses upon the school's way of building up children's achievement in school work organized in a core curriculum. And the intention is to extend the relationship between school and the community.

Teacher–child relations in daily school-life have typically changed in the direction whereby paying great attention to the children's ideas, reasoning and attitudes is usual. This perspective puts the emphasis in the classroom upon:

1. slowing down that rate of introducing new topics in instruction, so the children's 'already-given' experience and knowledge can influence the questions studied,
   and,
2. grounding work in the classroom mainly upon *deals* instead of commands; using more open questions instead of the more traditional ready-made tasks you will often find in textbooks and teacher-produced worksheets,
   and,
3. taking the problems of evaluation to be a mutual task for both students and teachers.

References

Borg, K., Florander, J., Jensen, K., Kreiner, S. and Moller, K. (1981). *Laerernes arbejdsmiljo i folkeskolen*. Copenhagen, DLF and DPl.

Gistettner, P. (1976). 'Handlungsforshungunter dem Anspruch diskursiver Verstandigung', *Zeitschrift fur Pedagogik*, Germany, no. 3.

Henriksen, E., Hesselholdt, S., Jensen, K. and Larsen, O. (1984). *Intervention og magt*, Copenhagen, Royal Danish School of Educational Studies, Pedagogy and Psychology 23.

Henriksen, E., Hesselholdt, S., Jensen, K. and Larsen, O. (1986). *The Democratization of Education*. Copenhagen, Royal Danish School of Educational Studies.

Levin, M. and Simon, R. I. (1974). 'From ideal to reality', *The Interchange*, vol. 5 (3).

CHAPTER 3

'A good place to grow up in'

The Laborschule and the Oberstufen-Kolleg, Bielefeld

'A good place to grow up in'

Susanne Thurn and Elke Werneburg

Background

In Bielefeld, West Germany, a school was planned in 1968, when Prof. Dr Harmut von Hentig took up his chair in pedagogics at the newly established university. It was opened in 1974. Since then, about 1400 pupils and students between 5 and 29 years of age have been working and living together in the school, which tries to realize some basic ideals about greater democracy in school life. Educational theory and practice are seen as developing hand in hand, and teachers are seen as doing their own research on their work with children and young people. The aim still is to find out which aspects of education are capable of innovative change leading to more equality of opportunity and to demonstrate the conviction that school can be humane – a place of experience – where pupils and students can learn and live together, not graded and with as little suffering as possible. The Laborschule starts at the age of 5 and ends after eleven years, and gives its pupils, after their tenth grade, all the different leaving-certificates pupils of other schools can achieve. The Oberstufen-Kolleg takes four years and tries to enable students from different schools, and young people who have already finished an apprenticeship and/or have worked for some time and/or brought up children, to study at German universities. It therefore combines, by special curricula and settings, a German '*Abitur*' with the basics of university study in the particular subject areas in which the students are interested.

Laborschule

The Laborschule was founded upon six basic theses, and in the discussion which follows, we will explain what these are and how we work with these ideas.

1. The first thesis is:

The function of school has changed in our century. For most children it has become a place where (necessarily) they have to stay most of their day. It therefore should be a place of living as well as learning, 'a good place to grow up in' (Goodmann 1971).

The Laborschule is built as an extended open area with as few walls in it as possible. Classes have their corner in it with, of course, tables and chairs, but also cupboards, bookshelves, games, handicraft materials, tea cups and a carpet to sit together on during assemblies or during teacher-directed lessons. Close to the corners are the zoo, a big cafeteria, small tea-rooms, a disco, rooms for making music and art, wood and metal workshops and laboratories for the natural sciences. Teachers also have their desks, their recreation corner and a place for drinking coffee in this area, amongst their pupils. Living together like this demands rules, which are established and accepted by all members of this community. Teachers and pupils know each other well, not only from their classes together but also from their behaviour with different people, during stress periods and leisure times. Teachers become persons, persons you can argue with or weep out a grief on, persons you can talk to, not only in terms of work but about all the little nothings of everyday life. Important barriers to learning can thus be understood and balanced. Learning and living together in such an open area also means that children are not at one teacher's mercy – they can look around, walk around, can learn from others as scheduled, and they can get new ideas.

2. The second thesis is:

If the school is a place to grow up in, children do not just acquire knowledge and skills in it, but also learn how to live. The life-to-be-learned should have the quality that life in our society has, or rather, might have. School ought to be a place where people realize differences, accept them and master them – and, in every way, it should be a place to accept the dignity of individuals.

660 children in eleven age-groups attend the school, half boys, half girls; 12–15 per cent are foreign workers' children; 55–60 per cent are lower-class children, 35–40 per cent middle-class and 5 per cent upper-class; 5 per cent of our pupils would otherwise attend a special school for educationally subnormal or handicapped children. Every age-group is divided into three groups, in which sex, class, national, or ability distinctions are represented as close as possible as in the school as a whole. There is no selection whatsoever of children according to their learning ability; different learning groups are founded only on interests and on choice. In practice, this means that teachers have to offer quite a lot of different ways of learning within a group. They have to make special provision for slow and fast learners, for the ones who learn abstract ideas easier and for others who need a lot of illustrative material. Children learn from one another, help each other, realize that they need different time and help to reach a basic goal, and that they are all different and can do different things well. The teachers try to give each child in a group what is the best challenge for him or for her.

3. *The third thesis is:*

School ought to be a place in which all members can learn how to live in community. On the model of this community, children learn the basic conditions of a peaceful, just, well-regulated and responsible life together – and all difficulties, obstacles and awkwardness caused by community life, as well.

Community demands a lot of order, of self-control and agreements on the aims and limits of relations – it also means getting a sense of solidarity, being stronger together, feeling sheltered, and having lots of fun with each other.

Social and political learning is as important as school-learning – and it takes quite a lot of time! Daily meetings of the group, especially for the younger children, are necessary to grow up into this kind of community. It is the children's meeting and it is mostly arranged by themselves; they tell each other what they have done during the day, they read their own stories to each other, listen to books, the teacher reads to them, they talk about their problems at home, or at school with teachers, or amongst themselves, with the bigger children and so on.

They try to find solutions and vote on them. They also discuss school projects and ways of developing projects. For the first three years of school, the younger children work in groups of fourteen. After that groups of twenty children stay together to share school life for the next eight years. It is the first and mostly the only group in their lives, in which they are so close together, escaping all the distinctions that separate them later in life. Learning politics goes on in different general assemblies of parts of the school or as a whole; it goes on, of course, during classes and in school activities, such as project-weeks, on topics like the world peace movement or contacts with our partner school in Nicaragua.

4. *The fourth thesis is:*

School ought to be a place where the *whole* person can develop, not just his or her brain, memory, or intellectual power.

The Laborschule tries to replace as much instruction as possible by experience, or at least, to complement it. This kind of 'all-embracing' learning is understood as a task of the school in order to adjust pupils to the shortcomings of our social life for as long as they cannot do it for themselves, and for as long as their lifetime habits are being built up.

This starts with the natural demands of their bodies: they don't have to sit all the morning on their chairs, they have a lot of opportunity to move around, a lot of sport, opportunities for dancing, playing, swimming; they learn better eating habits and, of course, sex is not a neglected topic. Their sense of responsibility is gained, for example, in the zoo, where they keep and take care of a small pet of their own, which also satisfies some of their needs for tenderness.

The school subjects are combined into what we call *Erfahrungsbereiche*: areas of experience. There are five of these areas:

1. people dealing with people;
2. dealing with things: observing, measuring, experimenting;
3. dealing with things: discovering, creating, playing;
4. dealing with your own body;
5. dealing with speech, writing and thought.

The first combines social studies, the second natural studies, the third the arts, the fourth games, sports and motion and the fifth, all language instruction. A new, sixth one is mathematics, which we formerly attempted to integrate into the above. In this way, things which are artificially torn apart without much sense are brought together again. Not until the last years of school are subjects crystallized in the process of specialization which is linked with the fields of experience.

At least once a year, the groups show parents and a wider audience what they have achieved: it might be a circus performance, a big exhibition of art, or a self-written play about the problems of youngsters; it might be a revue about one of their projects (for example, 'war and peace') or a lecture on their own stories or poems. Thus, not only subjects within one field are shown together, but often, more than one of the fields are combined.

What is important is what we call 'learning out of school', in the nearby university, the city, during excursions and journeys, of which we have one every year (the two 'big' ones of two weeks in seventh grade – skiing – and the ninth or tenth grade as the final journey to a foreign country).

A lot is done together with the family of the pupils: spending leisure-time or celebrating together are important and very difficult aims, which must be taught and learnt.

5. *The fifth thesis is:*

School ought to be a bridge between the conditions of living in a small family and in the big multitudinous systems of life in society – training, work, consumer systems; the government, control and power, traffic, communication and information systems and all the other different systems people have to cope with in their lives.

From what has been said so far, it is already obvious that our school gives these aims importance and time. But there are – besides growing up into community – other systems in between family and society which have to be learnt. For example: the small children visit their parents' working places with their class and they learn about their way of living outside home, getting to know extreme differences of circumstances. During the last three years of school, there are three periods of practical work outside school, prepared for and evaluated afterwards at school. During the eighth grade three weeks are spent in productive industries, during the ninth grade three weeks in service industries, and during the tenth grade placements are according to the pupils' own training plans for the future and according to their own choice.

At school, there is a school garden to look after, a kitchen to prepare and share meals together, a newspaper to be written, and also a library in which to learn and to relax.

The Laborschule is something in between home and the demands of society, demands which we try to prepare the children for – but in slow steps, depending on their development. We call this '*Stufung*', something like 'stepwise'.

First step: three age-groups (pre-school, first and second year of primary school) work and live together in their own 'house' in fourteen groups of all ages. This demands almost radical individualized learning programmes for every child in order to compensate for some of the extreme differences between them on their way to some common goals.

Second step: third and fourth year of primary school. The children are now in age-groups of twenty. For most of their school day, they work with only one teacher, but they now start with specialist teachers, sometimes in specialized rooms. They now start with English as a foreign language, they work in our workshops, and visit the facilities for leisure time.

Third step: the first three years of secondary school. One teacher is still in special care of one group and teaches his or her own group as much as possible, although the number of specialist teachers grows. The students regularly go to specialist classrooms and mix with other class and age-groups according to the courses they choose to study. About one-sixth of school time is spent on freely-chosen options. In addition, students can choose to learn a second language.

Fourth step: the last three years of secondary school. One-third of their classes are now in optional courses. This is their time for specializing in certain fields, their chance of gaining special achievements in one subject. They can show this with their work in performance courses and prove it in the courses as well, in papers or practical assignments, of which they have to hand in six during the last three years.

For the latter, they can also choose which teacher will supervise their work and judge it. During these three years there are the three periods of practical work–experience in industry, described above.

School work becomes more complex with this step, more is expected of the students, but it's more their own responsibility as well – this is what they grow on.

6. *The sixth thesis is:*

In the end, schools are still schools: a place to gain useful information, skills and qualifications.

Every half-year, the pupils get detailed reports on their work. These reports are supposed to describe their work, to explain special merits as well as shortcomings, and to encourage but also to warn those who don't live up to their best. In practice, a rather poor child doing his or her very best might get good and encouraging reports, while another quite gifted student might get some harsh warnings, that his or her work is below his or her standards of capability. Thus, we can do without grades or failures up till the last year of school. Then they have to face grades for the first time, get different leaving-certificates comparable to regular German schools. In our opinion, pupils have better chances than they would have otherwise, their certificates are of a higher standard than their family back-ground would suggest. Whether these certificates are really justified, can only be assessed in the future. The first age-group that left school in 1985, after attending it the full eleven years, is accompanied by a university research group to find out what every one of them has accomplished or will accomplish in life. The first results are quite encouraging.

Oberstufen-Kolleg

1. *Something about the 'Oberstufen-Kolleg' (OS) in general*

By its very nature and by design the OS integrates the final years of school with the first phase of university education.

Attendance is for the whole day and the school operates a varied system of courses and has places for 800 students. In a period of study lasting for four years, the students go from the first stage of the upper school level to nearly the intermediate exam stage of university in one or two subjects. The OS offers study in 22 major subjects ranging from history and law or psychology through music and natural sciences. After graduating from the OS, the student con-tinues the subject that he or she had chosen at the beginning of their study into the second to the fifth university semester. Being success-ful in passing the special examination of the institution, the students automatically fulfil the general university entrance requirement (*Abitur*).

At the end of the 1960s, when the OS was planned by Hartmut von Hentig, one of its main aims was just that: an alternative way to university. The development of the school took place at a time when, in the Federal Republic of Germany, the whole education system was under discussion. The basic ideals of realizing more democracy in school life were, at the time, to consider education as a right of every citizen, equality of opportunity, educational reform and the revision of curricula. In this context the OS developed a lot of unique outlines for its pedagogical situation, outlines concerning admissions, the curriculum, the learning and teaching process, the type of teachers and evaluation and assessment techniques.

1.1 ADMISSIONS

- the proportion of male and female students is fifty-fifty;
- of these, one-third have successfully completed the tenth class level of a '*Gymnasium*' (grammar school), one-third the tenth class level of a '*Realschule*', and one-third '*Hauptschule*' (both secondary schools);
- at least one-third of all of these have to have finished at least a two-year period of apprenticeship and/or employment;
- as far as social background is concerned:
  50 per cent come from the lower class;
  44 per cent come from the middle class;
  6 per cent come from the upper class;
- students must be between 16 and 25 years of age on entry into the OS.

So in the end students in the OS range from 16 to 30 years of age.

1.2 CURRICULUM

Didactically, the curriculum at the Oberstufen-Kolleg (OS) can be described in terms of the five types of courses:

- The OS sets out to make available to every student a planned choice of study area and later career, and for this reason, from the very first semester, she/he is faced with the necessity of working in a specialized field of scientific study. This is provided especially by '*Wahlfachunterricht*' (main subject options) which occupies 30 per cent of the whole study time.
- The OS sets out to offer the students a general '*wissenschaftspropädeutische*' education (study in the techniques of interdisciplinary scientific learning). This is covered especially by the '*Erganzungsunterricht*' (so-called supplementary study seminars), which occupy 25 per cent of the time.
- The OS sets out to give the students some experience of the advantages and limitations in interdisciplinary project-work.

This receives special attention in the '*Gesamtunterricht*' ('integrated group project study phase'), which occupies 15 per cent of the time.

- The OS tries to meet some of the demands for greater individualization of study by incorporating in each semester a period of individual study in order to help the individual to catch up in uncovered areas. This takes place in the so-called intensive phase: 25 per cent.
- The OS attempts to emphasize and safeguard the relationship between the kind of education it offers and the spheres of practice in the world outside; this takes the form of the '*Praktikumskurse*' (practicals). They occupy 5 per cent of the semester time, and in them the three required periods of practical experience in industry and society outside (each lasting four weeks) which have to be worked in the holidays and have to be prepared, planned and evaluated in the college.

Further specializations in the learning process are

- a wide range of different forms of teaching and learning (from small-group work to podium discussions);
- many different possibilities for students to participate in organizational and decision-taking tasks – from the shared planning of individual courses to the medium-term development of the curriculum, and in the operation of their '*Selbstverwaltungsgremien*' (own organizational committees);
- an alternative system of evaluation of achievement (pass/fail instead of grades or marks);
- a varied system of possibilities for counselling (in the whole of the '*Orientierungs*' – (preliminary) semester and counselling on subject-specific problems through a tutorial system).

1.3 TEACHERS

The 100 teachers in the OS can be differentiated according to their own education. There are teachers from school, men and women researchers, but all of them are both researchers and members of the University of Bielefeld and teachers at school. In their function as teachers they have three interrelated roles. He or she is first of all a teacher with responsibility for the various types of courses that make up the OS curriculum. In addition, the teacher must also be a researcher who is responsible for making a contribution to education through his or her work in curriculum development.

Finally, the teacher is an administrator as a member of one or more internal administrative committees of college.

2. *Some aspects of self-regulation of the college and of self-direction in learning*

Until 1980, one could find a very high level of self-regulation in the OS. The staff of the school managed nearly everything by itself, working formally with the Senate of the University of Bielefeld. But then a set of regulations was given to the school from the ministry of North Rhine-Westphalia which brought this arrangement to an end. Political and pedagogical life in the institution is ruled now by a *special examination*, by some *basic principles* (for example, for admissions, administration, co-determination) and the *administration organization*.

Nevertheless, compared with the ordinary school system there are still some good conditions for democratic self-regulation and the co-determination of the school. Nearly everything that is of interest to the school (budgeting, personnel questions, pedagogical process) is discussed and decided in the conferences of the school (meetings of major subject groups), in which teachers and students are represented half and half.

Besides that there is another committee that is occupied with special academic and scientific topics like research and school publications, where members of the University of Bielefeld participate. And there is, of course, self-administration by the students. The staff of the school attaches most importance to the question of whether there is a head of the school like a 'headmaster' (appointed for life) as all schools in Germany have, or whether there is an elected directorate chosen by the members of the school.

Though the basic principles from 1980 demand a head, the OS still elects a leader and three other members of the directorate for four years. And until now we have been successful in the fight with the ministry about this principle.

Personally, we would like to stress another aspect that is typical and important for democracy in school life. As well as their right to participate in the conferences of the school, our students also have the right to co-determine the process of every single course in their education.

Besides the chance of deciding the direction of political and pedagogical life in the school together with teachers in general, learning groups are integrated in the design and development of courses. Especially in the general study courses, there is frequent discussion of aims, topics and methodological questions at the beginning of the courses. Students participate in making decisions about the structure of the course, their way of learning (single work, work in groups, reports of teachers) and even about the special achievement system. Together with the teacher they decide which tasks they will have to fulfil to pass the courses. Course grades are 'pass' or 'fail', in contrast to the differentiated marking system used in other schools. Passing a course usually requires submitting written and oral work or, depending on the nature of the course, some kind of project involving a tangible product, experiment, or demonstration.

As far as we know, this right to participation is unique in our school system. We think it is revolutionary because the teacher is no longer the executor of the pedagogical process.

And what are the results?

As in other schools and universities today it is difficult to find the new members for the committees in the OS, and the more political students lament the inactivity of the majority of students and teachers (!). But nevertheless the self-regulation works. You'll still find at the school a very open decision-making process in all central questions of the institution. This takes a lot of time. In contrast to former days, today we find a tendency towards rolling back decisions from activity groups of teachers *after* they have been discussed for a long time in the committees. Democracy takes time!

The school research-study describes the results of co-determination more succinctly:

- 86 per cent of the students insist that teachers give reasons for their course plans,
- 92 per cent think that the plan of a course is determined by the members of the groups, and,
- 70 per cent said that they could integrate their personal interest in the courses.

The study also reveals that women especially have difficulties in influencing the plans of the courses and in talking in front of the group. The results show that co-determination isn't always achieved even if there is a formal right, but that the educational process depends on the continuous work of talking and motivation led by the teachers.

Fifteen years after the founding of the school, a new initiative started which, in my opinion, belongs to the demand for more democracy in school life.

In contemporary life some problems of society are emphasized, and yet the scientific system of the traditional social and natural sciences are evidently no longer able to address those problems. Problems like:

- the destruction of nature and the environment,
- the continuation of discrimination against women,
- the breakdown of the medical system (smashing the human being and fobbing it off with drugs).

Some groups of teachers rethought about real new ways of education. For the last two years we have developed three new studies at our school:

- ecology
- health sciences
- women's studies

which are not to be found in the traditional canon of the disciplines of the university. Their existence serves as a criticism of the traditional system and to emphasize the need for relevance in the practice of the sciences.

The new studies have not yet been really accepted by the ministry in North Rhine-Westphalia, but they are already planned and will be tried out soon. Then we will open the first two courses in ecology and women's studies with about twenty students in each course.

3. No democratic consciousness without women's studies

We emphasize women's studies, because current research has consistently suggested that girls at school and women students at the universities are still discriminated against, though formal equal rights and chances have been proclaimed again and again. Therefore, it is not only important to fight for additional funds and tenured positions for women but for new curricula, appealing to the interests and demands of women students. Otherwise women have little chance to find their own identity, which is important for our society to survive in the future.

Therefore, women teachers at the Oberstufen-Kolleg developed a programme for women's studies. The courses – interdisciplinary, and planned by historians, sociologists, psychologists and literature specialists and mainly taught by them in team-teaching – are part of the 'general' programme, that aims to combine political education and social learning with an introduction to academic research. The core of the women's studies programme are four so-called '*Kernseminare*' (main courses) which are compulsory. They include questions and topics such as:

1. Socialization and the situation of women today
    - the making of the 'true woman'
    - tracing one's real identity
    - discrimination against women
    - women's lives and literary biographies.
2. Women and labour
    - history – that is, 'her-story' – of sex-polarized division of labour
    - feminist social criticism
    - conditions of the development of the women's movement
    - present conditions of women's labour
    - professional activities and the forming of personal identity.
3. Women and culture
    - images of women in art and literature
    - women as artists, means and conditions of cultural production in our own and in other activities
    - the female artist.
4. Women and scientific research
    - how do various sciences define women?
    - how are women affected by the natural sciences and by technology?
    - feminist approaches to scientific criticism and methodology
    - scientific theories.

At these courses, women students participate in the production of knowledge. The integration of the 'female point of view' within scientific knowledge is a general demand of the programme, and that means that one focus is on participation in research work. To work in an interdisciplinary feminist academic way is one of the central principles in most main courses. The so-called 'objectivity' in academic research is opposed to the 'subjective view' of women, that includes intuition, dreams and fantasies.

Such a process of teaching and learning obviously requires participation by all members of the group and, as a prerequisite, a climate that allows the students the intimacy to talk about themselves, their own wishes and hidden desires.

For that reason the women's studies programme is not a fixed curriculum. It is a frame that can be reversed. The development of the programme is meant to be a continual process.

Let us give a glimpse of how this development works by describing some courses which have emerged.

1. WHEN BEAUTY CAUSES ILLNESS

This course dealt with the problems of women who suffer from anorexia nervosa. The students learned psychological theories concerning the development and reasons for illness, read biographies of sick women in that context and in the end talked about themselves; about problems with beauty, their bodies and sexuality.

Later, the group analysed publicity and advertising to do with women's beauty, thought about cultural differences (considering the Turkish women in the course) and took part in some psychological training, for example, fantasies about their bodies, and how to realize wishes.

2. WITCHES – YESTERDAY AND TODAY

In this course, Elke Werneburg worked, team-teaching, together with a friend, a teacher in historical art. Together with the students we did some research work in historical archives in Elke's home town, Lemgo, where from the fifteenth to the seventeenth century hundreds of women were burnt as witches. We read documents of those times and tried to find out the truth of the situation and everyday life of those women. The students studied theories about society, religion and human rights.

But we were all very interested in learning about witchcraft, magic potions and words and how they work in the contexts of human relations. An important theme in the course became our attempt to question our basic assumptions and prejudices.

3. FASHION – SELF-MADE IN OS

Bielefeld, the university town, is famous for its production of fashion, clothes and sewing-machines. The roots go back to the eleventh century. In this course the students did some research work about a well-known commercial house and participated in a traditional fashion show at a well-known shop in Bielefeld and looked for alternatives in the town.

Besides that, the group analysed and criticized the fashion market, which is generally controlled by men.

In the project course which followed, students designed and sewed their own clothes and dyed cotton. After that they organized a fashion show, in Paris, at a meeting for experimental schools in 1987, demonstrating self-made fashion in an alternative way for women.

In these courses we tried to find out what women really need in education. The results seem to be very simple but nevertheless include some real needs.

They need room for themselves where they

- have the chance to make new personal experiences
- are able to make decisions and real choices
- are able to think about new values, which are useful for women
- are able to reflect on their past and think about their future and visions
- are really able to be and live their own lives and emotions
- get to know that personal wishes and desires have a value of their own
- get the opportunity to be successful in their work

and above all

- to find teachers and members of the group who are able to talk and listen to them.

These women's studies courses have been validated by the Ministry of Education in North Rhine-Westphalia for a period of three years. Within this time the curriculum has to be evaluated, and its spread into other schools will be one factor used in assessment.

The future?

Since the two school projects at the University of Bielefeld were founded in 1974, they have had to demonstrate continually their efficiency and value to the ministry and often against public opinion, even in our own town. The last challenge for the schools was the retirement (*Eremitierung*) of their promoter, Hartmut von Hentig, at the end of 1987. But as far as we can judge today, the Ministry of Education and the Ministry of Science have both agreed to keep the schools in existence and that they can work their own educational programme for another decade.

Reference

Goodman, P. (1971). *Compulsory Miseducation*. Harmondsworth, Penguin.

CHAPTER 4

Schools without walls

The Villeneuve College

Colette Augoyard and Bernard Jardel
(translation by Linda Fisher)

1. The contract

The Villeneuve project, which was developed in a town near Grenoble, is characterized by a desire to forge a new basis for community relations. Villeneuve is a new part of Grenoble, built with the intention of bringing different socio-economic and cultural groups together in an atmosphere which would allow those living in the new town to create their own forms of social and cultural life. This basic intention is ambitious. Factors like the absence of a common language and the presence of cultural barriers, on the one hand, and a strong inclination towards individualism and a fear of other people, on the other, stand in the way of the basic goal of the project, democratization.

These obstacles – individualism and cultural diversity – were at the forefront of our minds when we began the educational strand of the new town development, the development of the Collège de la Villeneuve. From the very first step towards building the college – the recruitment of the people who would form the team to establish the new school – these conditions influenced our thinking. Not only was it essential to bring together educators and administrators who understood the aims and the obstacles involved in the whole project itself, but it was also necessary to work with certain specific ideas of the *kind* of people who would be most appropriate members of the team. Failure to effect a satisfactory recruitment policy was likely to jeopardize the whole project or to rob the experiment of its significance.

This being the case, we formulated a flexible, though very important, framework for our recruitment policy. We recognized that a democratization project makes different kinds of demands on those involved and that recruitment, therefore, cannot be done on the usual basis. First, all candidates need to be fully aware of the ultimate goals of the project, of their material work-conditions and of the ways in which they will be connected with the work and related to other team-members or participants. But this right is tied to responsibility; each application to join the project will constitute a kind of approval of the objectives set for the project and an agreement on the main lines of action being proposed. Secondly, because work in a democratization project is constantly changing and makes personal demands on those involved in it, it takes on the characteristics of voluntary service, of community work which reflects the concerns of different professional agencies. Thirdly, and in so far as the Villeneuve experiment is concerned, experimental work always places those involved in a new kind of relationship to established customs, to traditional ways of doing things. From the very beginning, the Villeneuve project was large-scale. It brought together several hundred educators (parents, teachers, youth leaders, instructors, social workers, community leaders, and volunteers) in circumstances which meant that they would be called upon to work closely with one another. It was an unprecedented operation which anticipated a wide range of educational and social changes. These changes would have to be achieved within the framework of French society yet also in opposition to specific customs of the society. These customs, under the cover of 'nationalism', tend to conceal rigid institutions, the long-standing existence of hierarchical structures and the application of social norms that work so as to relieve individuals of their personal responsibilities and to stifle initiative, imagination and creativity.

How, then, could the project be initiated in a way which fully implemented the framework we've just described and which opposes the established customs and norms without, in so doing, putting the entire operation at risk? It soon became evident to us that a very clear definition and statement of the anticipated outcomes of the project would be needed as the cement without which the whole edifice would tumble. To produce this, the New Town of Grenoble Commission, which has an established membership of between 120 and 150 individuals, was preoccupied with twin concerns: first, to find a basis for the constitution of the teams effectively engaged in the experimental project and, secondly, to plan the most favourable system in which this team could operate. The commission prepared a draft charter in which the aims of the project, the lines of action to be pursued, and the basic organization for participants were all defined.

For us, this charter was very important. It serves as the basis of the conditions under which everyone involved in the education programme in Villeneuve participates. It gives a starting-point for the specific roles of the various professionals involved and, although these roles will and do develop in the course of the project, the charter initiates new thinking, new definitions of professional obligations and work methods. And it articulates some of the fundamental ideas on which the 'action' side of the project was founded.

Amongst other things, the charter set out some broad perspectives on the kind of educational enterprise we hoped to develop in the new town, as follows.

Education

Education consists of a global action, an action which can no longer be divided into separate sectors and bounded areas, into periods of activity and of inactivity. Its ultimate aim is to help the child or the adult to become:

1. a person of judgement, capable of taking individual and collective responsibility, of assuming responsibility for oneself and always committed to a process of continuous self-development;
2. a sociable, creative being who is equipped with a decisive mind.

The role of parents in the education of children is essential. Parents and parents' associations are, at one and the same time, both key people in the process of education as global action and sources of knowledge for professional educators. For those reasons, parents are to be represented in the team of educators and we need to recognize that they will demand continuous support in their own education and development in their 'job as parents'.

Furthermore, professional educators must work together to refine their objectives and their methods and to inform parents of what they are doing. It is only in this way that dialogue and a continuous co-operation might be established between professionals and parents.

The notion of 'educators' obviously includes parents. However, only the professional (or voluntary) educators are bound by this charter. It is aimed at all those who influence training in and the integration of the areas of:

- health and social work, family planning;
- schooling;
- professional training;
- popular and continuing education;
- cultural action and leisure.

Teaching

Teaching is indistinguishable from education. It must aim for the harmonious development of all the abilities of the child and help him or her extend those indispensable tools of expression – oral, written, mathematics, audio-visual, aesthetic and corporeal. It must provide systematic help for the appropriation of knowledge and it must be linked to life; educational activities must integrate the experience the child has of life outside of school, in school and in the classroom.

This concept of teaching is also appropriate, with certain adaptations, for adults in the framework of continuing education.

The pursuit of the general goals, summarized above, necessarily involves a relentless struggle against a number of handicaps, a struggle which circumscribes the educational choices we might make.

1. The struggle against socio–cultural handicaps.
   The removal of those handicaps encountered by children from the 'disadvantaged' social strata of the population and a general raising of their potential for development are major objectives to be pursued throughout the life of each individual child, particularly during the decisive period of early childhood.
2. The struggle against emotional maladjustment.
   Most maladjustment and 'psycho-neurotic' troubles originate in the socio-familial context and are, in part, related to

emotional deprivation. This recognition gives particular importance to the close involvement of parents in the school process and makes the integrated co-operation of teachers, family members, psychologists, doctors and social workers an educational priority.

The essential spirit and the main formal objectives of the charter were legally enshrined in a convention signed by the prefect (préfet), the rector representing the Minister for Education and the Mayor of Grenoble on 20 December 1973.

'This organization', it stated in the Preamble to the Convention in a description of the community association from which the Villeneuve College would emerge, 'is a response to the vision of developing youth leadership, training and continuous education in the Cité through an agreed process of participation by closely associated educational, social, cultural and sporting activities'.

On the one hand, [it continued,] it intends to put into practice the full deployment of professional teams and, on the other, to realize the decentralization of public services and activities in a vision of permanent education which is not merely a pedagogic and economic necessity. It is a mechanism to secure equal opportunities *throughout* life, especially if such equality has not been achieved in initial education; it demands the opening up of schools and of universities to the community for the benefit of all citizens. On the basis of this vision, those in positions of leadership will not be able to accept the administrative roles previously associated with such status. Concern for the direction and integration of organizational units must be linked to a concern for community activists and their work, which is centred on cultural action and socio-educational action. The practical realization of these ambitions involves new relational structures between the whole of the school system, the family, the community and all organizations through which socio-cultural practice is born and nurtured.

2. The college

An original organization which favours the initiatives of the participants.

The college (or high school) which was born and nurtured at Villeneuve, as a practical realization of the aspirations voiced in the charter and the convention has a unique organization – a new democratic system. Diagrammatically, it looks like this:

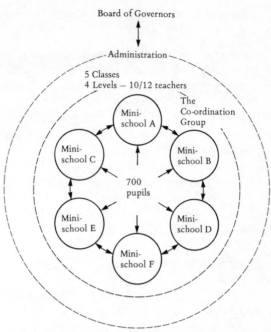

Figure 4.1 The organizational structure of Villeneuve College

But let us explain how this model actually works.

(i) The teams

Each teacher 'belongs' to several teams.

1. The team of class teachers (six to eight teachers), which is the real centre for excellence and guarantees the coherence of the teaching programme and monitors pupils' progress *in the classroom and at home.*
2. The team of 'mini-schools' (10–12 teachers from different subject areas) which draws up specific programmes within the framework of the global plan for the college and which manages and evaluates these programmes – to do with finance, the use of buildings, and the timetable.
3. The team of subject tutors (mathematics, French, etc.) – excluding specific vocational/apprenticeship staff – which tries to implement the multidisciplinary aim of the college.

The 'specialist' teams come together according to the skills and resources or the interests of each team, in relation to the needs of the college – and permanent interest groups, 'problem' committees, and research groups get established.

4. A co-ordination group – made up of the headteacher, one teacher elected from each mini-school, parents' representatives, educational advisers and service personnel – which meets every week to oversee the management of the whole college.
5. The general meeting, which takes place every three weeks, and brings together all adult personnel of the college and parents' representatives, to debate the necessary evolution of our school in a democratic forum. (According to subjects being discussed, pupils are sometimes invited to the general meeting.)
6. The board of governors, which provides the legal structures for the whole school, brings together representatives of:
    *   the personnel of the establishment;
    *   the parents;
    *   outside agencies such as local community associations and the world of work.
7. And the head of the organization? She ensures, together with the board of governors, the 'piloting' of the complex system and keeps watch over whatever statutory 'rules' are in force.

(ii) The classes

The management of pupil groups is flexible. The *basic* structure centres on the class group, but the flexibility of management in the *mini-schools* allows other groupings. Class groups can be divided or brought together for special purposes like workshops or vocational programmes. In practice, in the mini-school you might find a teacher-tutor working with just one pupil or demonstrating in front of several classes.

(iii) The timetable

The management of time is 'supple'. The organization of the timetable or of apprenticeship schemes for the pupils can vary according to subject, the interests of the mini-schools or particular projects.

Usually, the timetable works in terms of the 'lesson hour'; however, the 'light' administrative structure of the 'mini-schools' permits significant variations of weekly or even yearly programmes. Numerous apprenticeship activities, either for, say, a half-day or, for the duration of a long course emerge and timetable periods for any subject can be 'globalized' during the year, according to local or national policy.

(iv) The pedagogy

Pedagogic practices in a place like Villeneuve are obviously going to be individualistic and varied. However, to give some illustrations of how the basic ideological principles of the college are turned into actions in the real world of the classroom, what follows is a brief account of how things work in just one class, the English class for beginners.

3. The classroom – Collette Augoyard

The pedagogy in Villeneuve takes heterogeneity inside a class as a base. This principle was established by the Staff Assembly which, since 1973, has decided to form classes with pupils of varied nationality, of different social cultures, of different levels of ability, so as to work with a group reflecting the composition of our urban culture. This choice is now a structural and democratic necessity of how we organize our teaching. More than anywhere else, Villeneuve's area welcomes migrants from North and black Africa, the Near and the Far East and South America.

The language teacher is faced with a particular challenge here. I've been teaching English in Villeneuve since 1973 and for over six years now I have tried to introduce into my practice some educational innovations, linked to action-research, which address this challenge. These strategies can be classified as follows: those dealing with *knowledge*, with *skills* and with *behaviour*.

With respect to scientific procedures relevant to knowledge acquisition, democratization in language-learning implies, for me, the introduction of features of real life in the teaching process. One should be able to learn a foreign language as we learn our mother tongue. Casual observation of the child in the process of learning her mother tongue reveals that in building up her learning procedures, she uses multiple information. Basically, these procedures pertain to either the linguistic field or to the wider one of communication. Also, the information may be from aesthetical sources (linked to the five senses, space-motion and emotion); or, they may be from practical or manual sources. In daily life, data obtained from experience with the world of objects or 'facts' helps the child as much as that supplied by adults and peers through conversation and communication.

It is useful to recall here, two large currents of research which have given some valuable insights. The linguists of the School of Prague have shown that speech conveys a system of communication much more complex than is superficially carried in 'the message'. Similarly, the School of Palo Alto has suggested that any communication is inseparable from the environmental and social context in which it is produced. The body has as much importance as the message. Learning a language can be done both through the body and the use of space in a social context. Theoretically, these ideas have been developed by writers like Hall and Birdwhistell. For example, Hall (1966) studied how people use interpersonal space and distances in communication. He classifies these by four types, each alternatively used on a close or far phase: the intimate, personal, social and public distance. Birdwhistell (1970) analysed 'body emotions' in non-verbal communication. According to him, the body communicates various information by gesture, posture and relation. Gesture and posture can be defined in three smaller units such as the *kine*, the *kinem* and the *kinemorphem*. On a more general scale, behaviour is made up of three main types: the *instrumental*, the *demonstrative* and the *interactional*.

If one tries to work with these ideas, the language class can become a privileged place for knowledge, skills and behaviour to coexist and influence one another in the learning process. These ideas suggest new pedagogic possibilities, as well as giving more varied chances to a larger number of pupils. But, to bring forth these ideas into the classroom, certain conditions appear necessary. First, one must plan and build a space more flexible and more powerful than the traditional classroom space, then enrich that space through the introduction of data akin to that found in the 'natural' social environment.

My first concern has been to set up a new type of classroom space which contains all the familiar markers or signs of a child's everyday life and environment, then to bring into this space a sound environment which is related to this approximation of reality.

For example, take the Project of Educational Action (PAE), entitled *Space and Communication in the Language Class* (1981–2). The space conceived and built up here is the traditional classroom space, suitable for the transmission of knowledge for written work, either individual or in groups: it is the space appropriate for linguistic data and communication. At the same time, it is a more 'familiar' space, in which everyday speech can be acted. For this purpose we created the conditions of a home, into which we introduced some British features. The pupil is allowed and able to use the 'props' and arrange the space while learning and seeking information. The multi-functional and multi-form space was worked out in collaboration with the School of Architecture of Grenoble which gave special attention to the economy and convenience of symbols on the scenery.

Or, consider the project *Sound Environment as a Prompter of Communication in Language Learning*, (1983–7). This proceeded by changing the classroom–space into a more symbolic space, highly evocative of everyday life. That space which calls upon body, sight and touch has been enriched by the sound environment of the child's familiar everyday life at home. Using original sound cassettes created at the Research Centre on Sound Environment (CRESSON) at Grenoble, we built up a setting in which the children were immersed in a realistic sound context. This permits an *initiation* into listening, as well as a *linguistic learning* environment prompted by sound. In this way, the cassettes we use and play in addition to helping with *the learning of the sounds things make*, introduce the *sounds of actions* and the *sounds of made-up situations*, closely linked to a language learning progression. We then proceed from the simple to the more complex sound, and, at the same time, from elementary to more advanced language. First the word, then the clause, the sentence, the narration, the dialogue and the sketch are introduced by the sound compositions described above.

These innovative strategies have brought forth new relations in the classroom and new attitudes for the teacher, the pupils and the group, for it has enlarged the aims of teaching and of learning.

Teaching. The space makes certain demands on the teacher, on her personal ability to move, to introduce, to choose and to use information from everyday life – or, keeping to a theatrical metaphor, it challenges her to question the parts she has to play. If she is the main actor, under the spotlight, she is also the technician in the shadow, the prompter to communication and socialization.

Learning. To progress in the learning process, pupils are taught that they can use *any* pieces of information (intellectual, manual, aesthetical, or communicative) and start with those they prefer. No matter how they proceed in the learning situation, the aim is to come to a final production, written or oral. The variety of information gives *all* pupils a clue to start off any assigned task. This is of great help to 'remedial' pupils, who mostly need to stick to reality and to factual information.

The pupil is very often asked to share her knowledge with the others (the group). The whole class can be asked to do collective writing. Tasks demand, for instance, deciding what one is going to write or how one is going to respond to the situations composed for the sound cassettes.

Skill development is related to the progressive difficulties in the work the pupils choose. They may choose simply to write about the setting of the 'sound scene' (who? where? when? what?), or to do more complex sentences about the events and actions or about more elaborate lines of dialogue. Whatever they do, they must help their classmates if they are in difficulties – correct mistakes, take into account what others have written and enrich their own knowledge through gaining the knowledge of what others are doing.

Pupils can be asked to work in groups of three or four in the written or in the oral phase of lessons. Investigation in groups, then, is a *cultural* and *social confrontation*. To be successful, the group has to deal with its difficulties, for it is known that their final production will be evaluated (assessed) by other groups and the teacher. A heavy emphasis is made on the '*creating phase*' of *oral improvisation*.

A group is asked to 'perform' their response in front of others. The topic and the directions, given by the teacher, must be followed, and as long as the semantic field is observed, the group may manage the topic as they like. This illustration of the 'speech act' (Austin 1970) calls on the linguistic performance of the group. This is the phase in which pupils and teachers are able to appreciate the strategies introduced in the class. One notices that pupils take time to speak, to move: they hesitate while seeking information, they speak in inter-action with the other actors or with the class. With some of them the body acts before speaking: information follows the gesture. Some others take into account relationships first and give their speech emotion, humour and rhythm. Others make the linguistic message a priority and, by so doing, sometimes damage the quality of language.

All these episodes of the English class are followed by an *evaluation (the assessment) of the abilities required*. The linguistic field, the quality of the sketch (emotion, humour), the quality of the language (in-tonation – acting), the relationship between the partners and the parts they have taken are discussed by the class, the group and the teacher. To emphasize what has been successful, each different assessment item is taken into account and marked (plus/equal/ minus). If the group wishes, a mark out of 20 is given as well.

The English class, then, appears to be a place where one *learns how to learn* and *how to be with others*. It is a place where one can take the initiative, where body and mind are on the move. One learns at one's own pace, with the help of others.

If we aim at both teaching and socializing pupils, we must involve them *in the process of learning*. In the language class the pupils are in a situation of communication in another language. This must make sense to them. The innovative strategies lead them into the theatre of daily life, where everyone has a part to play. Gaining knowledge, taking initiatives and individual and collective risks become the basis of an education for active participation in future episodes of social life.

4. The future

For the last 15 years, the Villeneuve College has been involved in a process of progressive transformation. Intuitively, it has been able to forge its own history, that of a living entity in which various forces and tensions were given free play and sometimes caused real crises. Often the project relied on improvisation rather than planned development. Yet there have been some real changes, some real achievements.

On the credit side, we would want to emphasize a number of positive achievements in the process of transformation. Villeneuve is now an 'open' college – with no enclosed spaces and no fences; and out-of-class time can be used by pupils to go home, or to relax in the college social centre, or to use the *'médiathèque'* (media library). Villeneuve is also open to the community – with open access to the restaurant, to the *médiathèque* and the neighbourhood community centre. Villeneuve is itself a community college which offers various clubs and associations, courses and help with media production to everyone in the area. Villeneuve has established strong links between teachers and parents – through a home–school tutorial system, through an integration of welfare provision, and through the real involvement of parents in the general and the day-to-day manage- ment of the college. Villenueve has gradually developed a flexible and friendly organization for pupils to live and learn within; the 'mini-schools' of the college provide students with a small-scale teaching unit in which they can ask for changes in what is provided for them and can make comment on the global development of the college and in which teachers can experiment and innovate. But most of all, the college has gradually built up a fairly balanced system in which the people involved feel secure with the regular review and revision of aims, with experimentation and with taking on new roles.

But what of the future?

Though, from the outset, the educational project has centred upon the development of the child, as both a social being and as a unique individual, in the end, the aims and the strategies of the project are in the control of the educational team. The institutional context and the teachers' acceptance of this context mean that at Villeneuve, as at any other college, adolescents are first and foremost pupils who will be judged by the institution on the basis of scholastic performance. If this is so, can we say the college functions democratically – with such obvious differentiation of roles and power between pupils and teachers? Obviously not!

It is rather that the right to expression and initiative on the part of pupils is respected; it is up to teachers who feel concerned to find and maintain acceptable ways of guaranteeing this, and thus sharing some of their power. Acceptance and recognition of a right of expression seems a necessary condition for gradual progress towards the acquisition of recognized status and a system which is based on expressed and negotiated needs and not just designed by adults in the children's interest.

References

Austin, D.L. (1970). *Quand faire c'est dire*. Edition Sevil.

Birdwhistell, R. (1970). *Kinestics and Context*. Philadelphia, University of Pennsylvania Press.

Hall, E.T. (1966). *The Hidden Dimension*. New York, Doubleday.

CHAPTER 5

'Pedagogy of the oppressed'

The Kinkerhoek project

Claire Hülsenbeck and Tineke Smit

From 1971 to 1978 a project of educational innovation took place in Amsterdam, the Amsterdam Innovation Project (AIP). The immediate reason for setting up the project was the discovery that children in the older parts of the city – largely children of semi-skilled and unskilled workers – were lagging behind other pupils in terms of educational achievement: their performance at primary school was lower and only a few of them went to 'higher' (academic) forms of secondary education after leaving primary school. One of the first schools that participated in AIP was 'The Kinkerhoek' and that's why we are describing the educational programme in this school as an example.

Something about 'The Kinkerhoek'

The school is situated in a nineteenth-century, working-class neighbourhood. It is a primary school, which nowadays in The Netherlands means a school for 4–12-year-olds. The school has never been an experimental school, so there are no more facilities than there are in all the other schools in similar situations.

The pupils are from about twenty different nationalities. About half are Dutch and half are from ethnic minority groups. So it's a very multi-ethnic school and both teachers and parents are glad about that. The school reflects the population of the neighbourhood. For the Arabic and for the Turkish children there are special teachers (for education in their own language and culture). These children go to these teachers for about two and a half hours each week. The 230 pupils are divided into ten groups. This is done so that we keep the groups small, but now we face the problem that we have no teachers left for extra help. Only for one morning a week can we ensure that there are two teachers working with one group, and for these pupils that's not enough.

In the past ten years there have been a lot of changes in the neighbourhood of the school. Quite a few parts have been renovated and the population has changed rapidly. Most of the very old, poor houses have been pulled down and new houses have been built. Five years ago, a new school was also built. By community struggle a kind of 'integrated' building was raised, in which you find a school, a public library, a community centre and a sports hall.

'De Kinkerhoek' is a school which has been in a democratization process for years. For us this means, a school where:

- children see what their own world has to do with knowledge;
- children get insight into what is learned and why and how they can apply what they have learned to other situations;
- children get insight into the learning process.

Thematic teaching

Democratic education in Amsterdam schools like the Kinkerhoek is centred around a *theme*, chosen from daily life and from the neighbourhood in which the children live. The kind of democratic education which starts from here is given shape in a didactic scheme in which we distinguish three phases: *awareness*, *collecting* and *ordering*.

We call this way of teaching *thematic teaching*. When any subject-matter is systematically integrated into the chosen theme we call our method: *theme-course teaching*. The methods we use in our didactic scheme came from everywhere: from Montessori schools, from Jenaplan schools, from the British infant school, from Freinet schools, and from the American Centre schools. Some methods we invented ourselves in AIP, particularly the idea of themes starting in the neighbourhood and in the reality of pupils' own daily life. And, of course, the didactic scheme was also invented in AIP.

Where do the themes come from?

As we have already said, the themes come from daily life and from the neighbourhood of the school. Children are learning, by asking questions about a theme, by researching, and by broadening their experiences in this way.

1. The most common way of finding a good theme, is in the Kinkerhoek itself: to pull it from a theme that was 'done' before (there are always new questions left even when you have found your answers).
2. Many themes come from real life – newspapers, television, festivals, seasons, parties and so on.
3. Children themselves can propose a theme by bringing up things they want to research, or by bringing up a problem, an experience or a feeling.
4. Teacher's choice is also a possibility. There are always themes a teacher wants to introduce and in the Kinkerhoek there are many themes which frequently return, like 'Apartheid', 'Your Free Time', or 'Working'.

Different types of themes

In the Kinkerhoek there are three types of themes:

1. A theme in which a democratic attitude is discovered, discussed and developed – a theme about a special democratic skill. There are themes like 'Helping Each Other', 'Quarrels and Solutions', or 'Being Friends'.
2. A theme by which the environment, the society, the world is explored. Democratic skills and attitudes are developed by work methods like working in pairs, in gender groups, or in language groups, and so on.
3. A theme which, when complete, leaves something behind in the school: a custom, a democratic way of organization. This third type of theme can best be illustrated by the 'post office theme', which typifies our methods and our goals.

The post office project

This project originated when a new post office was opened near the school. It was an interesting point for children of all ages, so it became a theme for the whole school. We went to have a look into the post office, at the opening. After discussion in 'the circle', the children wanted to get more information upon how the post office worked. At the end of the project we built our own post office in the school. Children understand how it works, how to address letters, to stamp them, and to order and to deliver.

We opened our school post office with an opening party. All the children in the school joined in the opening. One of the parents even made up a song for the new post office and all the children learned to sing it.

Even now, after two years, our post office still works. It's open nearly every school day. Pupils can mail their postcards, drawings and letters to their friends and teachers. During the morning a child from an older group goes to a younger group to find a younger child with whom she/he can act as 'postman' together. They empty the mailbox, stamp the letters, sort them and deliver the post in all classrooms. All our children like this 'job' very much, so we have to organize it in turns. They also like writing letters and receiving them. So this is a good way to practise reading and writing. Another very good thing is that they can use it to say things which they find difficult to tell somebody. Frequently, teachers hear about the little (or even big) problems from the children through the post office. Thus, we can say that knowledge of the '*postoffiche-projekt*' has been integrated as a school custom and with a lot of democratic aims being realized as a result.

Which themes are done in the Kinkerhoek?

In the Kinkerhoek, themes are either *existentially oriented* (themes like 'Who am I?', 'My Home') or based on social critique ('South Africa', 'Squatting'). The last kind is mostly worked out with the 10–12-year-olds. Criteria for the acceptance of a theme are: has the theme something to do with *living*, *working*, or *leisure*? Extra criteria: are there any links with *geography* or with *history*?

The 4-year-olds start with themes about themselves, their bodies, their clothing, their pets, and so on. As their world widens they become interested in themes around home and the street, like being ill, the market (because there's a market very near the school), the park, and so on. Around 10, they start producing and choosing themes like 'Amsterdam' and what to show someone coming from somewhere else, or being unemployed.

When the children are interested in world-wide themes, we make a distinction between: *World 1* (nearby or psychologically very near –

like 'Peru', because one of the pupils went there and sent us many letters about the country and about life there) and *World 2* (the 'really far away' world). Themes, then, might emerge as illustrated below:

Criteria	Living	Working	Leisure
myself	who am I?	being ill, getting well again	your free time is your own
home	the kitchen	time	I play home
street	squatting	market	to the park
city	Amsterdam	labour	drugs
country	sex	energy	tourism
World 1	Morocco	unemployment	pocket money
World 2	South Africa	Nicaragua	tourism

The didactic scheme

In the following explanation of our didactic scheme, we'll use some examples from a project 'Being Ill, Getting Well Again' to illustrate both the stages of the scheme and all our methods.

1. Awareness

In this first phase the children are given an opportunity to become aware of their knowledge about the theme, their feelings, and their experiences.

The main thematic aim in this phase is: motivation of the children and the discovery of common reference points in the group. The main democratic aim in this phase is: the children are getting insight in and grasp of the learning scheme (the didactic plan). After some time these children are able to influence their own way of learning more explicitly and more frequently.

In every phase we have a package of didactic methods and of ways in which the group of children can be organized. The grouping strategies are as varied as possible, given the situation in school. We work in pairs, in groups based on gender, language, interest, or friendship.

The methods of the first phase are:

(a) A STARTING EXPERIENCE

A starting experience can be a film, some slides, a visit by a parent or someone living in the neighbourhood of the school, a book promotion, or some other kind of 'real' stimulus.

If this isn't enough to help children see the opportunities contained in the theme or to get motivated we introduce some extra methods like: 'Tell me your associations when I say . . .'. Or like playing in a '*centre*' which is specially made for this theme.

> *Illustration:* The teacher (Tineke) chooses this theme 'Being Ill, Getting Well Again', because one of the pupils fell ill and had to go to hospital. (There were children between 6 and 9 years old in this particular group.)

(b) THEMATIC CIRCLE CONVERSATION

This group–discussion is the moment when every pupil has to give words to his/her experiences and feelings and then to discover the *differences and the similarities between him/herself and the other pupils. At the end of the discussion which questions are left is noted and it is decided which of them are important enough to research. The teacher has the difficult task here of both listening and of trying to give things a structure: this is the starting point, the level of knowledge from which education has to depart.*

> *Illustration:* So many children seemed interested in being ill and in hospitals and they so much liked to talk about their own experiences that we decided together to use this as a topic.

(c) SEMANTIC FIELD

A semantic field is a short notation, in single words, of what is said during the thematic circle conversation. Through experience in thematic circle conversations, our pupils soon learn to formulate what's the really important thing and what's not. Together, they make one thing the centre of this semantic field, the basis for the main decisions about learning during the whole of the next period, for which part of the theme is to be worked out first and which part isn't important at all.

Because of the fact that The Netherlands is a multi-ethnic society nowadays, we make room in this phase for mother-tongue talk. Of course, children who need this are allowed to speak their mother tongue in the 'centres' or in the language-group, but in group-discussion *every* pupil has to face the point of different languages, and the consequences of living in The Netherlands today.

Every pupil makes a translation of the *semantic field* in his own language-group, the 'white' pupils making a translation into 'street' words. After this, everyone writes an essay, a poem, or a story in two languages, the dominant language and one of the other ones. If somebody needs a word that's not on the semantic field he/she can inform him/herself in the language-group which specializes in mother-tongue language. This method is one of our first steps on the way to equality of languages and of pupils in the classroom.

If there is time enough or if it's necessary to help pupils achieve the aims of this phase we also have some extra methods which are not 'standard', like drama, free writing, and so on.

> *Illustration:* After the discussion, I asked the children to make a semantic field out of our circle-discussion on the topic. From looking at this semantic field, lots of questions were raised.
>
> *Extra methods:* We decided to work things out first and the children mentioned symptoms, diseases, and also a lot of parts of the body. Some children painted a body and we named all the parts. The next step was to mention what's the result of having a broken leg, or missing any other part of one's body during some period of time. In their 'body book', they wrote sentences like:
> 'My legs: without legs I can't walk.'
> 'My lips: without lips I can't kiss.'
> 'My fingers: without fingers I can't pick in my nose.'
> So the children first start by exploring what they already *knew about the theme;* after this we could start collecting new information; there were certainly enough questions left.

2. Collecting

In this second phase of the didactic scheme, the pupils learn to broaden their experiences, to discover a wider world, and to learn, thereby, new knowledge and skills: they collect new experiences because all learning starts here.

The main thematic aim in this phase is exploration of a wider world. The main democratic aim is: acquiring skills like curiosity, assertiveness, initiative, confidence in one's own abilities and in the possibilities of working together and helping each other.

Didactic methods in this phase are making interviews, collecting information from the library, exploring the neighbourhood of the school, playing and working in 'centres', looking at films, photos, slides, going to a museum, asking somebody's parents for information, inviting people in the classroom to tell something about the theme, or whatever. In this phase we tend to operate in language (mother-tongue) groups rather than in the teaching groups – not through choice, but because of the resource situation in the school.

Illustration:

Outside collecting   To get the answers we were looking for, we decided to pay a visit to a hospital. Of course, the children liked to see the children's ward. They could ask a lot of their questions there.

One of the children asked about having a broken leg, so the nurse showed us the plaster room. A child brought her doll with her and a male nurse dressed the doll's leg in plaster.

On another day, an ambulance came to the school. The children were allowed to look inside. One child was taken into the classroom on a stretcher to show what happens when the ambulancemen have to take a patient down these steep and narrow Amsterdam staircases. Or, somebody came to tell more about the school's first-aid kit, about its contents and use.

Inside collecting   The children could find more for themselves in the *book centre* in the classroom. In a special '*look-up centre*' we made task-cards with information about the theme.

3. Ordering

In this third phase pupils are learning to get a grasp of the information they have collected in the second phase. New skills must be developed, new knowledge has to be integrated.

The main thematic aim in this phase is: integration of information and flexibility. The main democratic aim is: insight into a grasp of power relations, and ways of promoting action.

Methods in this third phase are all the traditional ones and a lot of new ways of training and of acquiring knowledge like mathematics (especially working with schemes, diagrams and plans), writing a report, a play, making an exposition, and so on. The *ordering* phase always ends up in a circle-discussion, where everyone shows his or her productions and where appointments are made about the consequences of all the research done.

Illustration: In our school, *ordering* can sometimes be done in groups, another time it's done individually. For 'Being Ill, Getting Well Again', we had many ways to choose from:

- simulating in our self-made hospital (a new centre in our classroom)
- playing in the *world-orientation centre*
- playing and writing in the *construction centre*
- playing in the *dolls centre*
- writing stories or poems, or making books
- working with word-sheets or with task-cards.

So, that is the didactic process at Kinkerhoek – awareness, collecting and ordering. And then we start again!

CHAPTER 6

Schools for the community

The democratic school – the successful school

Elia P. de Almeida

Introduction

In Portugal after 1974 there was renewed hope of providing success-ful schools for all children and young people. Steps taken in various fields and alterations made to the organization and the curricula of schools were designed to enable them to teach democracy and gradually to become democratic institutions. Democratization, however, cannot be reconciled with the unsuccessful school.

The percentage of academic failures has indeed fallen since 1974, yet we are still a long way from a school for all and it is often still the case that failure penalizes children from social sectors whose cultural background differs from that offered by the school. The number of failures seen in primary education alone shows social and cultural discrimination.

The situation has not changed much over the last few years. Thus, in 1982, 60.5 per cent of pupils in compulsory primary education reached our standard of educational efficiency – although, it has to be recognized that 28 per cent of pupils finally successful in their sixth year did, in fact, repeat the year for two or more times.

In 1982–3, the level of failure in primary education was 35 per cent, with higher values in the first stage than in the second (41 per cent and 27 per cent). Consequently, large numbers of pupils stay in school for many years, with teaching methods not adequate for their age nor their situation as 'educational repeaters'.

In 1983–4, in primary education (four years of schooling, starting at the age of 6), 5.9 per cent of the population was 12 or 13 years old and 0.5 per cent was 14 and above. In 1984–5, the numbers were nearly the same: 5.8 per cent, 12 or 13 years old; 0.5 per cent, 14 and above.

On the other hand, and according to the law, children are only compelled to stay in school until they reach the age of 14. So, a large number reach the leaving age and give up school without success-fully completing the sixth grade. And finally, related to school success, there are great regional differences, with poor results in the interior and northern districts of the country.

It is important that a quick solution is found to this problem – especially problems of failure in the first two years of schooling, as this seriously affects overall pupil progress. For those studying this area, the main difficulties occur in *transitional* years – from 'primary' to 'preparatory' and from 'preparatory' to secondary – and only about half the pupils who begin 'primary' education reach the tenth year of schooling.

Research undertaken has identified reasons for this lack of success but, as yet, decisions to alter the situation have not been forth-coming. Moreover, with the exception of certain specific cases, the school, in its daily life, is little geared to change. Most schools almost always ignore their socio-cultural environment and, locked within themselves, follow centrally-determined programmes. The text-book is often the main teaching aid and activities are given priority according to the status of the knowledge they transmit.

However, throughout the last two decades various factors have introduced some changes into the Portuguese education system. Of these, three are particularly significant.

- an increase in attendance at 'preparatory' and secondary educa-tion, three times more pupils between 1960 and 1985;
- the replacement in 1975 of the four-class system in primary education by one of two stages of learning, lasting two years each;
- also in 1975, the unification of the first three years of second-ary education, thereby delaying the time when pupils choose vocational and academic options.

As a consequence of these changes, those children and young people the traditional school overlooked – 'different' children – have progressively begun appearing in the new single type of secondary school. But, good intentions were not always turned into action. In parallel to increased growth there were gaps in quality and research, and legislation to correct the situation lagged behind the changes.

The Comprehensive Law on the education system

Since all political sectors have recognized the importance of improving the Portuguese education system, a new Comprehensive Law establishing the guidelines for organizing the new system was published in October 1986. According to this law, compulsory education, which had previously lasted six years, was extended to nine years, and this will apply to children entering primary school in 1987–8. This will obviously give rise to changes in the school population.

Article 2 of the Comprehensive Law established that 'the democratization of education aiming to guarantee the right to fair and real equality of opportunity' in both access to and success in education is to be encouraged. Thus, difficult problems involving the existing network of schools and the possibilities of success they offer will have to be faced, if the individual progress of each child and young person is to be promoted. Only then will collective progress be possible.

To encourage and to support individual progress a true understanding of each pupil is essential in a school, awareness not only of what pupils don't know yet and what they still have to learn, but also seeking to promote and enhance the school itself by using the abilities of the pupils in school development. 'Real equality of opportunity' means recognizing the difference, diversity and equal merit of all talents, whether pupils have developed them within the confines of the school, or not.

All societies are in fact multicultural, even in a single nation and a small country: being a rural inhabitant of the plains or the mountains, living on the coast or in the interior, in a city or a village, is to be different to some extent. In a single nation, multiculturalism is also a source of wealth for the society as a whole.

Culture implies a tradition of specific inheritances, yet it also refers to present achievement – with its own knowledge, its different points of view, and different expectations and motivations. Only a school which allows for such differences will cater for the real pupils it has accepted.

On entering the primary school, such differences are immediately visible. There are no ignorant children, even at 5 or 6 years of age. Often they simply do not know what their teachers would like them to already know when they first arrive at school. They can hardly hold a pencil yet they can play flutes they have made themselves and they recognize birds by their song. To learn how to read and write does not mean they must lose this knowledge, which is to be exchanged for the knowledge of others. Number 5 of the above-mentioned Article 2 stipulates that 'education furthers the development of democratic and pluralist ideals which embody respect for others and their ideas and is open to dialogue and free exchange of opinions'.

Respect for the ideas of others and a free exchange of opinions demands that the school should also be made to recognize, accept and enhance different forms of discourse. It becomes difficult for the school to adopt this attitude, attempting both to further the success of the pupil and to avoid the progressive destruction of cultural diversity. Teachers themselves are sometimes unaware of these values. Forcing children in a class to follow an almost uniform range of subjects, in what might be termed an 'anonymous' way, leads to collective impoverishment. There are many cases where the school, being unaware of everything the child is and everything he knows, and by trying to teach everything as if it were new, is faced with insurmountable difficulties and fosters an erroneous idea of culture. On the other hand, the child who is accepted by the school collaborates in the tasks allocated and, in collaborating, learns and progresses. To a certain extent, therefore, it is essential, even with pupils of a single nation, for the school to be multicultural.

Three situations

Following approval of the Comprehensive Law, certain actions necessary for preparing the corresponding regulations have been taken since the end of 1986. The newly established Comissão da Reforma do Sistema Educativo (Steering Committee for the Reform of the Education System) has been carrying out studies and drawing up recommendations consistent with the guidelines defined in this law. These studies are concerned with the organization of the curricula, the content of syllabuses and with school materials. However, they will have also to be concerned with the ways in which children from different environments learn, an area about which we still know very little.

The work of the committee has provided an opportunity for publicizing certain efforts and experiments which have been carried out occasionally, quite often only in one school or only in the class of a single teacher.

Lisbon

A good example of this work is the case of a small–scale experiment carried out in 'mother-tongue' learning in the first three years of a secondary school in Lisbon. In this experiment, there were two principles:

- That awareness of the environment surrounding the school and particularly of the environment in which each of the pupils lives is a way of getting to know them better, and this is, therefore, an essential precondition for the appropriate organization of working methods in the school.
- That one of the reasons for failure lies in the breakdown between academic discourse and daily life.

Classroom activities, without altering the established programme, are marked by the importance attached to the preservation and development of subjects and forms of expression of the pupils.

First, and concerning curriculum content – as a first step – we had to identify the themes in the programme that could or could not be treated in a regional perspective: childhood, school, work, meals, celebrations, seasons, the landscape, animals, men and women in the community. When dealing with these topics, the student identified with the environment he/she is familiar with, he/she uses his/her own words and values and compares domestic speech against school language. So, instead of avoiding language preferences, as a sign of difference, they go forward knowing them better.

With respect to the form of teaching, the study identified several aspects of regional speech-phonetics, morphology, phrase structure. At the same time the teacher-researchers identified peculiar features of language which do not follow the norms and relate to different usages and cultural patterns. Step by step, though 'home language' was accepted, pupils were taught language awareness and 'correct-ness'. They wrote down different registers and could gradually distinguish between popular and literary forms and uses of language.

When pupils have understood the importance of their contribu-tion to language study done in the class, they can be encouraged to research and take notice of characteristic forms, and involve families in this work, as frequently happens.

However, the particular attention each pupil is given benefits his/her academic results and integration in the class. Frequently they volunteer to talk about their own 'things' and not only to answer when questioned. On the other hand, projects like this reinforce the school–family relationship and the interests and motivation of families do contribute to the diversity of these periods of free talk: news of parties, announcements of celebrations which have gone unnoticed, fables explaining the colour of a stone or the flow of water, games which only the children of former days could teach modern children, recipes for meals tasting more of the country and the river than of the supermarket. Many families who now live in Lisbon, as well as acquiring the characteristics of urban inhabitants, have retained many features of their original environments which determine their actual, small-family world. These backgrounds could be parts of Africa or the plains of Alentejo or hills in the North. Yet the child and particularly the adolescent will only divulge this great wealth of little treasures if he knows they are being heard, appreciated and valued, even if the person who told the old story or invented the refrain which is sung in the religious procession is an almost illiterate grandparent, because there are illiterates with a vast cultural background. The school has a great deal to learn – even from these people. Furthermore, studying language, particularly oral language, which at times varies in vocabulary, phonetics, or syntax, gives rise to learning which is much more closely connected to real life than some of those examples sealed within a grammar book for years.

Many of the pupils involved in this project, who have so much to say that is different, are those who, if not given such attention, may appear shy and apathetic and even seem incapable if it is not accepted that they have a right to speak in their own way. The work carried out helps the progress of the pupils as a whole. There is no more simple and efficient way of teaching the plurality of Portuguese culture and the wealth of the language. Particularly important, however, is the interest and enthusiasm of the majority of pupils who, surprisingly, discover that each of us always has something to teach and much to learn.

The most difficult educational battles are those fought over the massive content of the syllabus, as if it were intentional to allow no room for real experience, or over the inflexibility of timetables incompatible with the rhythm of creating and planning.

Oporto

Another experiment has been taking place since 1980–81 in a 'preparatory' school in São Mamede de Infesta on the outskirts of Oporto. The initiative was taken by a group of teachers who were

dissatisfied with the way in which work in the school was developing: one day the same as another, de-motivating both pupils and
teachers.

In front of the school, in an old farm, there was a granite chapel, in
ruins, which has been turned into a hay-store. The chapel had been
standing there for centuries. But nobody looked at it.

In 1980, when talking about baroque art, a history teacher visited
this eighteenth-century chapel – S. Felix de Picoutos. The intention
was that students could see the main characteristics of baroque art, in
the field. For the first time, they noticed how dilapidated the chapel
was. It had to be saved. But how could they do this? This was the
origin of a school project which since then has developed along the
following lines:

- The work done at school provided enough material for an exhibition about baroque art. Why not in the chapel? It was held in the
  chapel.
- The owners of the farm agreed and the youngsters cleaned up and
  set the chapel in order.
- Weekly, on small trips in the neighbourhood (Oporto,
  Matosinhos, Leça do Balio) students and teachers improved the
  study of the baroque by visiting other monuments.
- The exhibition in the chapel drew the attention of the community
  and local authorities who were made aware of the value of this
  building.
- An invited architect spoke to everyone about his particular
  art.
- As a result of written submissions presented by students and
  teachers, the chapel was classified as a municipal monument and
  later on was bought by the council.
- Many other cultural activities were born in the school.
- In 1983–4 the Leisure Time Centre of the school was started.
  There are students and teachers interested in cultural activities
  such as theatre, dance, history, handicraft, drawing – they meet at
  the centre.
- Pupils went on picking up several objects from the past that were
  studied and exhibited: lanterns, clocks, pottery, farm equipment,
  toys, lace, embroidery, pictures, clothes.
- Some newspapers published texts by pupils and teachers about the
  necessity to preserve the chapel.
- In 1984 there was an exhibition about local Christmas traditions
  collected from the oldest inhabitants. A nineteenth-century rural

Christmas supper was held – furniture, clothes and food were prepared by parents and teachers together.

- One night this newly recovered treasure was the goal of thieves. They tried to steal the gilded wood-carvings from the shrine of the chapel. But the school watchman was there. And they had to run away.
- In 1985–6 the school studied Portuguese ornamental tiles. And, once more, they researched, studied them in the country and took some photographs.
- In 1986–7 help was forthcoming from several parts and the work of restoring the chapel began. The plans for this were drawn by an architect who is also a teacher in the school.
- Today, a technician on gilded wood-carvings is teaching the youngsters; they are learning how to categorize, how to classify, to treat and to restore the gilded wood-carvings from the baroque shrine.
- This year, to celebrate the 600th anniversary of the Treaty of Windsor sealed by the marriage of the Portuguese King John I to the English princess Philipe of Lancaster, pupils are preparing a representation of the marriage procession, making a great number of little figures. The work must be finished by June, to celebrate Queen Elizabeth's anniversary.

Minho

The last experiment to be used in this illustration has been going on since 1979–80 in the 'preparatory school' of Lordelo (Minho) in an area where agriculture is a subsidiary activity and much of the population (85 per cent) is employed in the manufacture of wooden furniture. Very young children themselves work as helpers. In this case, the stimulus for the project, was a group of teachers worried about high failure and drop-out rates. It was obvious that school did not arouse pupils' interest and could not solve the existing problem by itself. Many parents viewed the school as delaying their children's arrival in the labour market, as an obstacle to their children's futures. According to them, the school taught non-useful things, far from the world of work waiting for pupils outside in the real world – the wooden furniture manufacture.

The main objectives of this project were:

- At the level of the whole school
  - to promote democratic attitudes by equally valuing school knowledge and manual work;

- At the level of the pupils
  - to find the way of occupying leisure time;
  - to find room for self-fulfilment;
  - to link theory to practice;
  - to dignify local history and reality.
- At the level of the parents
  - to help them appreciate full compulsory schooling;
  - to make them understand and accept the school's goals and methods;
  - to realize how useful they themselves are to the school.
- At the level of the community
  - to develop awareness of professional training needs.

We can pinpoint the following main steps of the work undertaken by the school to meet these objectives.

1. For a full school-year, a group of teachers studied and collected all the necessary information about the history of Portuguese wood furniture (taking into account different influences and how we developed an original style).
2. Afterwards, they analysed the characteristics of the industry in the region and its needs and qualities.
3. Then, they discussed how to interrelate knowledge from the different school subjects with practical knowledge and the real world.

But only community involvement could provide the answer and give life to a real project. So this one was designed:

1. to get to know the environment (consider the complaints and suggestions of parents, meet cultural groups, study the history of the area so that knowledge of the past would help to understand the present better);
2. to welcome new teachers arriving each year, to integrate them into the environment, help their personal training, and plan activities with them;
3. to find space for occupying free time: open workshops dedicated to work with wood (wood carvers, cane weavers, etc.); for one afternoon each week, involving theory and practice under the training of a carver-craftsman from the community;
4. to study problems related to the daily life of the population;
5. to reconcile environmental needs, the objectives of education and pupils' needs.

A principal difficulty was the mobility of the teachers: one year's stay in the area (the norm here) does not make for profitable participation.

Results have been clearly positive. The community seems to have realized that the school belongs to them and that therefore they should be concerned with what goes on in·it; they realize that what schoolteachers do is important: and they see that their work also matters to the school itself. Students have developed skills, knowledge and values; and so citizenship is learned and promoted at school.

The school:

- is now living in dialogue with the community;
- is now trying to promote a true regional education;
- now feels that it is teaching useful things because teachers work with pupils they truly know, and they are confident in this area of work;
- now sees that the quality of teaching has improved; there has been a progressive fall in the number of drop-outs and the level of failure has fallen spectacularly.

And the future?

A school museum of wood furniture is their ultimate goal.

The democratic school is the successful school

All the above could, in fact, be summarized in a few words. The democratic school, the successful school, should be based on the pupil, and should know how to integrate itself with the environment in which it exists, and to understand that knowledge is only meaningful when it is part of real life.

These are simple words which do not contain anything new. However, one of our greatest writers of this century – Almada Negreiros, who was also a remarkable painter – wrote in 1921: 'When I was born the words which will save humanity had already been written, and only one thing was missing – to save humanity'. Concerning the school, it is just the same.

Reference

Negreiros, A. (1971). 'A invenção do dia claro', in P. Estampa (ed.) *Obras Completas-4*.

CHAPTER 7

Creeping democratization

Peers School

Pat O'Shea

Introduction

This case study describes curriculum change in an ordinary school. It illustrates how change in the structure of the curriculum and in the organization of the teaching staff can result in benefits for students: giving them equality of access to all parts of the curriculum, a higher degree of control over what they study and learn, and allowing many more of them the experience of success – including, but not exclusively, greater success in public examinations.

Peers School in Oxford is a 13–18 comprehensive school that was formed in 1968 from the merger of a grammar school and a secondary modern school which already existed on the same site. It is markedly different from the other schools in the city in that it serves the large municipal housing estates built for the car workers at the nearby factory. It has higher proportion of working-class and disadvantaged children than other schools in the city. Relatively few children stay on at school past the legal school-leaving age of 16. While the car works used to be a major employer, new technology has largely removed that source of employment, and many school-leavers now find work in service industries, especially tourism and catering. The school is not, however, in an area of high unemployment.

It has not been set up as an experimental school, nor has it had a great deal of attention from researchers. Several of its staff have been teaching in the school or its predecessor for many years. It is thus a well-established and stable school. However, since 1983 it has undergone a period of rapid and far-reaching change.

How change happens in such a school raises several issues. In particular, four issues bear on any debate about processes of democratization. They relate to teachers, structural change, the curriculum, and the school system.

1. Teachers

The culture of teaching is a powerful one. It is a truism that schooling is a process of cultural reproduction; at its simplest, teachers re-create in their work their own experience of schooling. Conservatism and tradition are inhibiting factors in any reform. All school reformers have to recognize that the staffroom is where change must happen. None of the other potential initiators of or blocks to change – parents, employers, the local authority, governors, even government legislation – can have as much practical effect as the teaching body.

The most pervasive model of teaching in English secondary schools has two main features: first, teaching implies transmission of knowledge from one who knows to one who does not; secondly, knowledge is divided into subjects, one of which is what a teacher teaches. The curriculum structure, as well as the career pattern of many teachers and a good deal of their professional satisfaction, are built upon these subjects. The issue, therefore, is how can teachers be persuaded, encouraged, or carried along to work for innovation?

2. Structural change

Innovation in schools has often begun by determining the nature of the relationships which should operate in the school, and therefore by looking at power. At Peers a different approach was taken. It was the structures that were changed: the new structures that were set up were enabling ones. Changes in teaching methods and in relationships could follow from them, but because such changes were not the starting-point people felt less threatened. The question then arises, how effective is a structural approach to innovation in a school?

3. The curriculum

We can think of the curriculum traditionally as rather like a 'black box' in an aircraft. Its contents and mechanisms are concealed from parents, from students, and even from teachers. Learning outcomes are measured by the crude instruments of grades at public examinations at 16+.

One major intention of the reforms in the curriculum at Peers School was to open up this black box – to be more explicit to all concerned about what skills, knowledge, concepts and experiences the various components of the curriculum would provide, and equally to be clearer and more consistently positive about the learning achievements of each student.

Whether this makes the curriculum more democratic is open to debate. As we will see below, the new structure made the curriculum more responsive to students' needs and interests; but control of what goes into the curriculum still ultimately rests with teachers: they determine what will be in the offer from which students make their choices.

4. The school system

However successful an innovative school is, it may remain isolated in terms of the school system as a whole. Some innovations have eventually had effects on substantial numbers of mainstream schools or education authorities (the Cambridgeshire Village Colleges set up by Henry Morris in the 1930s are one example), but others are perceived as oddities, to be tolerated or not as the case may be. A number of experimental schools have been the subject of destructive attacks from the media and elsewhere; others are marginalized. The question that needs to be addressed is how successful innovation in any one school, and particularly democratizing reforms, can transform practice in the school system as a whole.

The context for change

There is widespread unease in England about the curriculum, and particularly about the curriculum offered to adolescents in secondary schools. This concern is now being addressed, for good or ill, by the government with its proposal to introduce a national curriculum. But in 1982 this was not in prospect, and teachers at Peers School, like many others, were dissatisfied with the traditional curriculum.

They doubted its capacity to meet the needs of many of the students in the school, to respond to changes in opportunities for work, and to tackle issues of disadvantage arising from social class, gender, or race.

A school like Peers, run by a local education authority as part of the state-maintained sector, faces a number of issues in contemplating change. Attitudes to reform in schools, as noted above, do not always inspire courage. When numbers of students are falling, schools are in competition to keep up their enrolment, and anything that could shake parental confidence is risky. Moreover, funding was contracting faster than numbers; there would be little available to resource new developments. With an established staff, there would be training needs to be met; would the local authority support the initiatives? Such a school has to safeguard the educational outcomes for students; that is, however critical we might be of the examination system, we still had to be sure that our students would do at least as well in examinations. Indeed, believing that working-class children were underachieving in the present system, it was a high priority to enable them to do better.

Despite these factors, the determination to improve the experience of school for our students was strong. The need for change is best understood by looking at the context in which comprehensive secondary schooling arose in the late 1960s, when the basis for the present curriculum structure was determined. Since that time little has happened to shift the definition of educational success away from that which held sway before comprehensive reorganization.

In the post-war period in Britain, until the late 1960s, secondary schooling was run on a selective system. In most areas of the country, children were tested at age 11. Those who passed the test attended grammar schools. Those who failed attended secondary modern schools. The pass mark was fixed so that the number of children who passed exactly matched the number of places available in grammar schools – generally around a quarter of the school student population.

The system was reorganized by the Labour government of the 1960s under Harold Wilson. There were a number of reasons for this reorganization: the testing at 11, based on IQ, had been discredited; the marked difference in status between grammar schools and secondary modern schools disadvantaged three-quarters of students and affected their teachers; and the harmful effects of labelling children failures at the age of 11 became clear.

The selective system was divisive not simply along lines of

'intelligence', but along lines of social class. The number of work-ing-class children attending grammar schools was very small, although winning a 'scholarship place' was often seen as a route out of the slums for that minority. Thus, when schools were re-organized, the Prime Minister Harold Wilson announced that the new comprehensive schools would offer 'a grammar school educa-tion for all'. It is against this legacy that we are struggling twenty years later. Many teachers would agree that the curriculum usually offered to young people in our secondary schools produces disaffec-tion, rejection, and in some few cases open rebellion. The massive machinery of the public examination system dominates secondary schools and makes the experience of schooling one of failure for large numbers of young people: over one-third of examination courses embarked on by students at age 14 lead to no successful outcome. What has gone wrong with what started as an idealistic intention to offer the 'best' to all?

The curriculum of the grammar schools was very little different to that outlined in the official reports of the nineteenth and early twentieth centuries. It focused on scholastic, writing-based subjects, taught in ways which emphasized the transmission of received knowledge: English, mathematics, languages (including Latin), his-tory, geography and the sciences. It neglected practical, creative and vocational learning. It offered this curriculum to the quarter of the population deemed fit to receive it. When schools became com-prehensive, often in the face of opposition and accompanied by the traumas of merger and closure, the new schools were judged by the standards of academic achievement of the grammar schools.

The grammar school curriculum continues even now to exert a strong influence on the comprehensive school. The subjects of that curriculum are the ones which carry high status; the teachers who teach them, too, are often perceived to have higher status than teachers of practical or vocational subjects. Even more pervasive is a definition of 'ability' which is deeply embedded: students can be labelled 'more able', 'less able', and, most damningly, 'average', without any attempt to specify what abilities are being referred to: able to do what? Of course, implicit in this terminology is the understanding that 'able' means 'good at the academic subjects of the grammar school curriculum'. Many schools offered the majority of students a watered-down version of this curriculum – European Studies for those unable to cope with foreign languages; Combined Science instead of physics, chemistry and biology; often, bizarre subject names invented as euphemisms, such as the CSE examination entitled Maths for the Living. The legacy of the grammar schools is a curriculum which is inappropriate for many of those who receive it.

Most British secondary schools have a system in the later years of compulsory schooling which requires students to choose among a range of subjects: the option system. Students' choices are constrained in ways intended to ensure balance. The result of this system is a curriculum structure which differentiates along lines of perceived ability, social class, and gender. Students make their choices at the age of 13 or 14 and are then locked into these choices until they leave school at 16. Whole areas of experience can be dropped at 14, cutting off many career routes. Students are sorted into those taking academic or practical subjects according to 'ability'. Girls take home economics and drop technology; boys take metalwork and learn no parentcraft. Some of these two-year courses lead to a public examination qualification, others do not. The effects on motivation for the (inevitably less prestigious) non-exam groups are dramatic.

The critique of the curriculum outlined above would be agreed by many in education in Britain. In the specific conditions of the late 1980s, we can add to it two further factors: (i) increasing pressure to add new subjects to the curriculum without removing old ones, to take account of changes in working patterns: computing and technology are the obvious examples; (ii) the sharp drop in the numbers of students of secondary school age, which led to pressure on the curriculum as schools had to lose staff, and as group sizes fell making many subjects not viable.

These factors, together with the growing recognition that the 14–16 curriculum fails many young people, create the context for innovation. The catalyst at Peers School was the appointment in 1982 of a new headteacher, who was expected to initiate changes.

Curriculum change

The first stage of change was to reorganize the staffing structure. In 1982 there were some twenty departments in the school, each with a head who derived his or her status from identification with the subject and its status in the school. A head of department would fight doggedly to defend her subject's territory: rooms, staffing, capitation, timetabling. With falling rolls, competition between departments looked like becoming ever more bitter, as subjects were cut and departments shrank. Teachers' traditional allegiances to their subjects had damaging effects on them and on the school.

Recognizing this, the new headteacher regrouped staff into teams responsible for broad curriculum areas. It then became necessary to determine the time allocation for each of these areas. This time allocation is the same for all students, no matter what their age, their gender, or their level of attainment: this is an important principle, at present rare in British secondary schools, as it ensures that no student can drop out of important areas of experience. The time allocations which apply in Peers School were determined as follows:

English	12.5%	Community Studies	30%
Mathematics	15%	Creative Arts	12.5%
Science and		Tutorial	5%
Technology	25%		

Staff in curriculum areas were given blocks of time with whole year-groups, and asked to decide how the curriculum in their area was to be delivered. It was as a solution to this problem that the idea of a modular structure arose.

A module or unit of work lasts eleven weeks – about 25–30 hours of class contact time. It has very specific learning objectives, and is designed to include a range of teaching and learning styles. At the end of a unit there is an assessment, so students get immediate feedback on how they have done. Students are asked to evaluate their own performance, too, and to set themselves learning targets for the future. In addition, the school is part of a national records of achievement scheme, and all students when they leave receive the Oxford Certificate of Educational Achievement. This certificate, awarded by the Oxford University examination board, records achievements of all kinds, in school and out, is wholly positive, and has a section written by the student recording whatever the student wants to say about what they have achieved and learnt. This certificate is owned by the student, who may choose to show it to potential employers, for example.

Credits achieved in modules are accumulated, and at 16+ the best of these are selected and submitted for a public examination quali-fication (formerly, O Level and CSE; from 1988, GCSE). Only the student's best work need count for assessment purposes. A poor grade in one unit need not affect the overall final outcome.

In Science and Technology, for example, students take fifteen credits over two years, selected from about seventy available credit titles. Thus, although all students must spend a quarter of their time in this area, individual students have a high degree of control over what exactly is studied and learnt, provided their route-ways permit them to reach their targets in terms of examination outcomes. (Appendix 1 shows a sample student route-way through the curriculum.) These route-ways can be very flexible. There need be little prescribed content; instead continuity and coherence are achieved through careful planning of the skills, processes and concepts that students will encounter, whatever content is the medium for them. Modules are designed with this in mind: the same learning objectives can be met in many different modules. (Appendix 2 shows a sample module.) Students may follow their interests, and, if these interests change, they are committed only eleven weeks ahead. They have short-term goals to work for, which most students find improves motivation, and the very act of choosing creates greater commitment. Some constraints operate: all students must take some technology credits, for example, but the choice is wide, from jewellery to micro-electronics. In this way the traditional gender-stereotyping of technology as an area of study for boys has virtually disappeared in the school. The national figure for girls studying technology to the age of 16 is about 5 per cent; at Peers it is 100 per cent.

A modular structure requires teachers to be more explicit to students about what is to be learnt, and about the assessment of what has been learnt. Students are more accountable to teachers, because of the pressure of the eleven-week time-span, but teachers are also more accountable to students, in terms of delivering what they have offered. If a unit does not interest enough students, a teacher will have to offer something different. Popular units can be repeated to accommodate all takers. The curriculum is thus responsive to the pressure of student choice: individual students control their personal routes through the modular curriculum, while as a body they have an influence on its overall content.

The damaging effects of teachers' allegiances to their subjects are reduced, while the positive ones can be emphasized. Teachers can be reskilled: a traditional needlework teacher, for example, now also teaches Textile Technology, and units on textiles as part of Creative Arts. Her status is enhanced, but no longer comes from running a small department competing with others. Her skills are valued wherever they have an input into the curriculum. Teachers can develop units of work in topics they know and are enthusiastic about, many of which could not have been sustained over a two-year course – for example, the Science and Technology programme includes a few units of geology, taught by a geology graduate whose particular skills are thus put to better use. Since the exact list of credit titles may vary from year to year, the school can make the best use of the available teaching staff, while the time allocations in curriculum areas remain constant.

The future

This type of structure is new in British secondary schools, though a version of it has long been in use in parts of the American education system, and in Britain the Open University is organized on modular lines. Its application to secondary schooling in a very few schools such as Peers has attracted a high level of interest from teachers and educationists, and teachers with experience of working with a modular curriculum are in great demand for in-service activities as many other schools plan their own ways forward to curriculum change. While Peers is unusual in having a modular curriculum for all students occupying the majority of the week, other schools are considering adopting partially modular arrangements. They may do so for a variety of motives, which may have nothing to do with advancing democratizing processes. Using Colin Fletcher's analysis of three possible arguments which can be advanced for democratic change, they may do so because such models appear, from the evidence from schools like Peers, to improve the *efficiency* with which learning happens. They may do so from a belief that democratic reforms provide *enrichment*, as civilizing influences on the citizen. More rarely, perhaps, the intention is *empowerment*, or the clearer articulation of participants' rights. However, it is possible to argue that whatever the motivation of the institution for such changes, democratization is likely to be a result. This follows from giving students more control over their own learning, both through offering choice and through developing self-assessment in the context of greater explicitness about objectives and outcomes. Delivering the curriculum in modular form entails negotiation between student and teacher; and it requires teachers to change their practice through curriculum development and through more open methods of assessment. Hierarchical staff structures can also be challenged, and younger teachers offered the opportunity to be involved with planning and developing the curriculum rather than being handed ready-made syllabuses to teach (it is a much less daunting task to devise a 25-hour unit on an area of expertise than to plan a two-year course).

The power of the public examination system and its capacity to act as a dead weight on secondary schooling has already been alluded to. Once one begins to think in terms not of a two-year course leading to a final examination, however, but of a series of credits accumulated over time and combined to give a GCSE pass, one begins to see a way forward. Credits, after all, do not have to be gained in school. They could be gained later, through adult education, evening classes, or colleges of further education. Continuing education which offers worthwhile accreditation becomes a real possibility.

With this in view, schools and colleges in Oxfordshire have negotiated with an examination board that the accreditation of units of work for a public examination need not be tied to age. Thus, the credits for any given GCSE could be accumulated over a period of time before and after leaving school, and in more than one learning institution.

In conjunction with the examination board Oxfordshire has established a 'credit bank'. This is a bank in two senses: first, participating schools and colleges who develop credits have them approved by the board and then deposit them in the bank for use by any other member of the consortium, a promising example of schools collaborating over curriculum development. Secondly, students who have taken credits while at school may 'bank' them and add to them later credits taken elsewhere. At present there is no limit as to how long credits may be stored and added to, providing qualifications in their own right or accumulating to make GCSEs. In this there may be at least the potential to challenge the powerful tradition of examining at 16+, a tradition which has strangled many curricular innovations. This tradition also means that there is a very high premium on success during the years of compulsory schooling; while it operates, attempts to open educational opportunities to those who did not reach their potential at school will founder. Democratization can come through a structure which offers more people the chance of educational success, and which acknowledges people's right to valued and valuable learning; that means a much broader definition of achievement than schools have been used to.

Appendix 1: sample route through the Peers School curriculum

In 1986–8, one representative student called Susan took the following units of work. The credits obtained were combined as shown below to give passes in the new GCSE public examination. Alongside the title of the credit, where appropriate, is shown the traditional subject area to which the content of the credit most closely corresponds.

GCSE Physical Science with Technology and
GCSE Biological Science with Technology

Gears and Gearing	(physics)
Metalcraft	(design)
Dyes and Dyeing	(chemistry)
Social Biology	(biology)
Working with Materials I	(technology)
Technical Graphics	(technology)
Health Science	(biology)
Working with Materials II	(technology)
Food Technology	(biology)
Textile Technology	(technology)
Energy and Energy Resources	(physics)
Photography	(chemistry)
Pollution	(chemistry)
Life Cycles and Genetics	(biology)
Domestic Electricity	(physics)

GCSE Integrated Humanities

Beliefs	(religious studies)
Persecution and Prejudice	
People and Work	

These three units are compulsory for all students. In addition, for this GCSE Susan chose two units from:

The Community
Law and Order
Conflict
The Mass Media
The Family
Inequality

GCSE History
Historical Enquiry (compulsory)
Russian Revolution
First World War
Development of Medicine
Nazi Germany
History of Energy

GCSE Creative Arts
Creating a Scene   (drama)
Creating a Character   (drama and art)
Rite Electrik   (dance)
Play Production   (drama)
Barnum – a musical   (mixed media)

GCSE Business Studies
People and Communications
Word Processing
How Business Works
Business Enterprise
Clerical Duties
Information Processing

GCSE Mathematics
Two-year course with short-term targets built in.

GCSE English
GCSE English Literature
Two-year course incorporating short courses selected from a variety
of menus on offer. During the course Susan chose to study:

Speak Up!
Roll of Thunder Hear my Cry (a novel)
Looking at the Media
A First Look at Shakespeare
Power of Words

Appendix 2: sample unit of work

For each unit of work, a summary sheet is prepared as below. The
unit is described twice, once as it appears in the syllabus for approval
by the board, and once as it appears in the booklet issued to students.
This unit is one of 70 in the Science and Technology programme.

Title: Pollution Code: C36

1. Specific learning objectives for this unit (based on a grid giving
   criteria for different skills and processes at four different levels):

   C3 Makes accurate observations
   D2 Can carry out a sequence of procedures confidently

E2 Can read scales with sub-divisions
G2 Can give valid explanations using familiar concepts
I4 Can clearly and succinctly describe what he/she is doing
J4 Can produce clear written accounts in own words

2. Syllabus description
   What is pollution? Water pollution; study of factors affecting purity of water sources, eg suspension of particles, bacteria, pH, detergents. Cleaning water for domestic use. Over use of fertilizers, etc. Oil pollution. Disposal of car oil. Air pollution – filtering air, lichen survey, measuring sulphur dioxide and carbon dioxide from fuels, car exhausts, cigarettes. Effects of secondary smoking. Sulphur dioxide and acid rain on plants. Carbon monoxide on blood, lead poisoning. Noise levels and legislation to control pollutants. Sound proofing houses and reducing noise levels.

3. Description of content for student booklet
   Will we survive? Are our streams, rivers and oceans being poisoned? How clean is the air we breathe? What are the dangers of nuclear power and waste? Test our water supply and the air around us. You will learn about noise pollution and the effects of cigarettes. Is the future of our world as grim as some reports indicate?

4. Special resources needed: Sound meter

5. Visits planned: Sandford Sewage Farm

6. Links with other modules: Acid rain covered in less detail in C34; Fuels.

PART 2

The debates

CHAPTER 8

Democratizing research

(i) Iceland Wharf: action-research and educational innovation

Knud Jensen

Introduction

This paper is based on research experience gained as part of the Iceland Wharf project, described in Chapters 1 and 2 of this book. A basic goal of this project was the development of democratic relations between researchers and teachers, between teachers themselves, and between teachers and pupils (Jensen 1984 and 1986; Larsen 1986).

A central concern of the paper is how to avoid manipulation in projects of educational innovation and research. In the Iceland Wharf project we tried to develop procedures through which everyone involved – researchers, teachers, pupils and parents – agreed on the perspectives and priorities for the project and did not try to hide things from one another. The emphasis was upon returning to public discussion issues which had been previously kept private.

Analogies between research and innovation

Action-research is a process, and it is necessary to work with the methods and skills used on two levels. One level involves methods and skills used to analyse the process itself, and the other involves methods and skills used to promote strategic perceptions and policy (Touraine 1982).

In action-research – at least when it is linked with educational innovation – theory has to be of a preliminary character. This does not mean that one is without theory – just that one is prepared to make necessary changes in the theoretical field right from the start.

While the aim in research in general is to find new, unnoticed aspects of phenomena or events, the typical aim in educational innovation is to make direct changes. The combination of those two aims, to discover and to make changes, can be found in some projects within the frame of educational innovation and action-research. But, one has to be careful not to force analogies too far. Teachers are not first and foremost researchers, and researchers are not responsible for meeting the needs of the pupils. However, to some degree the role of the teacher and the role of the researcher might be demystified if their work and methods are seen as similar.

Teachers are the main agents of innovation

It is the teacher who has the greatest potential capacity for innovation in a school. Even if the teacher has no direct influence on legal aspects or on the economy, she has some power. Take, for example, the situation in Denmark. The Danish School Act is traditionally a political compromise. It is a framework for daily activity but so open to influence from teachers and students that they can arrange changes in actual practice and, thus, put some of their ideas into action in a direct way. Even if a whole staff cannot agree on a proposed change, it is sometimes possible for a group of progressive teachers to form a faction and work with say, democratic perspective in the everyday life of the school and the classes. And this has to be done even in spite of any resistance which might exist among their colleagues.

In a very simple form, this means that the struggle *on* the hegemonic ideology takes part *in* the ideological state apparatus itself. The parties might only discuss questions about ideas, rituals, routines and customs. In itself this will be a big step forward. Until now, many progressive teachers have not demonstrated their progressive ideals through small-scale experiments with new routines or with changes in ritual and school traditions.

This initial step is interesting from a democratic point of view. It could be said, in fact, that the establishment of fairly small changes in school ritual, routine and custom which are based on a democratic ideology is a necessary part of the whole process of developing democratic schooling (Vilmar 1973).

A common and agreed perspective

The ultimate goal for the Iceland Wharf project was to achieve the greatest degree of democratization possible – a goal for both the research element and the innovation element of the project. Until recently, we have consistently avoided making a consideration of an overall *concept* of democracy the crucial concern in the development of the perspective employed by researchers and by teachers. Although there are many arguments in favour of such an approach, we have found – in both analysis and in practice – that we are involved in an enterprise in which the power structure is being levelled, in which power is being redistributed and wound up. A key problem in this kind of action-research, then, is not the negotiation of agreed definitions but of building working relationships *inside* the project; or, to put it another way, to find ways of reducing alienation, the alienation of teachers or of pupils.

This reduction, to some degree, can be achieved:

- when the actions of the participants are co-ordinated around *agreements* to fulfil basic aims, whether these have to do with literary, manual, or artistic actions;
- when the achievement of these aims and their utility is evaluated both in relation to the interests of *individuals* as well as in relation to the plans and outcomes agreed by the *group*.

Educational innovation

Changes in participants' perceptions, their actions and their evaluations are the first steps in innovation. A teacher with some experience will know what a school day can be. In innovational work, efforts are made to enlarge such experiences through work with new ideas and new ways of doing things. Experienced teachers give qualified advice concerning in which direction it is possible to make changes.

But experience can also form a barrier to change, especially if one builds conclusions only from what is already known, and if one has had no experiences of the possibility of changing rules and routines by making new arrangements.

In educational innovation one can find that the search for change operates on several levels. One of these can be to look for other ways of working in the same direction, and to try to reach the same goals more rapidly. The intention is to promote, adjust and vary the methods one is accustomed to using. One is looking for new possibilities within well-known frameworks. On the other level, one is looking for changes which can shatter one's realistic experiences. The participants are looking for new and undreamed-of possibilities, as might present themselves when they are using a whole new perspective as a basis for their thinking about their work.

It is necessary to take both levels seriously and to link them together if the innovative work is to have a chance of achieving real change of practice and outcome. This should be obvious when the perspective is the development of an all-round educated student in a school under continuing democratization. If, during their school life, students are going to be more and more qualified to participate in decision-making, in reaching agreements, and in taking real responsibility, then it is necessary that they can 'see through' the code of the school and the perspectives the staff are working on. Basically, this means that adults themselves become familiar with the practice and perspectives in the school, so that they can then make them transparent for pupils.

Action-research means participation in development

Action-research demands that researchers not only explore behaviour and action but also take part in innovation and are at the disposition of the main agents in a project. If this is not the case, then action-research is reduced to exploration by some of parts of a process which is implemented by others. This makes novel demands on the researcher; he or she is engaged and involved in elucidation and description and in the negotiation of new perspectives. But, of course, involvement must be loyal to what is agreed upon. Therefore, the researcher has to be open and frank about his or her own attitude to the project.

Two arguments in favour of looking upon teachers as research workers
The teachers' working conditions

How does a group develop its capacity for decision-making on its own terms? It has been mentioned earlier that teachers constitute the active part in innovation, partly because of their position in the system. In many cases, research cannot be carried out without co-operation between the research-worker and the teacher, and often this co-operation depends on the teacher's working conditions. It is, therefore, important in educational development that the teachers are aware of some key problems in their own situation, otherwise it might be difficult to work on changes at all. The problems are:

- to change 'an impression of something' with insight, for example, about how to earn a salary;
- to change public problems which are felt to be private back into public problems, for instance, the matter of stress at work;
- to guarantee that the individual's opinion can be made public, for example, in the process of decision-making.

The character of innovation

The process of development work resembles that of other work processes, that is, that it can be described as consisting of the same sequences and phases as one can find in all work. Each sequence and phase can also be evaluated during the process, and this evaluation allows for corrections to be made while the process is still running. Due to this, recognition of what is happening is of great importance, and normally teachers are the only people who have the chance to 'see through' what is happening and why it is happening, and it is their observations which guides them to suggest changes within a process already running. The teacher has the chance of examining her interests, the amount of resources used, how opportunities and access to them were brought about and which actions were effected. And she has the chance of finding out how participants stand in relation to these variables.

The areas for research

For discussion, it is possible to distinguish research-areas in which teachers can obviously have an interest, along the following lines.

(a) One can identify that part of the teacher's work which goes on in the classroom, that is, didactical, social-psychological, or micro-sociological problems.
(b) One can identify those circumstances and conditions outside the classroom which determine parts of the teacher's work.
(c) One can look upon the important area outside the school, for instance, the neighbourhood and the living conditions and life-styles of the community.

The Danish Teachers' Union has taken an initiative of embarking upon a general campaign which, in addition to development of school work, also aims to renew the relationship between school and community and teachers' working conditions. Research concerned with teachers' work has often been carried out by researchers, but the use of these investigations has given some problems either because of the difficulty of using results in a single school, or because the results were collected to get a picture of teachers' working conditions, not to make changes or to mobilize for change.

Exactly the same problem arises with classroom observations, if these are made with the purpose of making only a description and not with a view to making changes.

We do have some social experience of teachers achieving educational innovation without direct contact with researchers. The problem here is how to develop aspects of systematic and scientific theory and methods into the staff's consciousness. The more one tries to establish autonomous and democratic learning situations, the more interested the teacher becomes as a researcher, because the teacher can ask why and try to find out the reasons behind the desire for change. The teachers also have the chance of distancing themselves from participant–observers in two ways:

1. longer periods of contact with pupils;
   and
2. power to change inappropriate processes and goals.

The great benefit of recognizing this strength of the teacher in action-research is that one can reduce the use of power, and through this also work with increased participants' influence. This type of research is not neutral, but, on the other hand, a democratic view on education does not mean that *everybody* should take part in decisions on what has to go on in the lessons. On the contrary, it means that those who are participating and doing the work take the decisions. You can exchange opinions on perspectives and framework, but you cannot let those outside take the final decision on what is going to happen. Let me try to give a few examples of research methods which can be given and taken over by teachers, so as to extend work on a school's development.

Within the sphere of thinking about teaching methods

It is of importance to make all the views of all participants public for discussion and constructive criticism. According to their ages and experiences, the problem in the classroom is to get students to present what is in their minds and to try to work actively to establish the possibility of them realizing their conception, or to change the goals of a project. The relationship between the researcher and the teacher is of the same nature, namely, to get the teacher's conceptions so public that they can be described, discussed and transformed into actions. This procedure is very like that facing students and teacher. It will be possible, therefore, to adjust the scientific methods to be used in the relationship between students and teacher.

Within the sphere of working conditions

In Danish schools, division of work is partly a matter decided by teachers' council. Very often, teachers find it difficult to carry this discussion all the way through, partly because individual teachers find it difficult to discuss their colleagues' work, that is, the strain of work and the division of work in public.

In the Iceland Wharf project, we tried to overcome the problem by carrying out an investigation of how work was actually divided. I doubt that this traditional quantitative examination in itself gave any new information to the staff. But to bring the results back for discussion opened the possibility of dealing with the problem normally placed in the teacher's minds as a private problem as a matter of public interest.

Within the sphere of relations with the community

For some years there has been a continuing discussion concerning how relations between the school and parents could be developed. The quality of this discussion has been marked by a high degree of generalization of concepts. Parents often talk about teachers as if the teachers were only roles or positions, and, the other way round, teachers often mention parents as if they formed a homogeneous group. Very early in the project the researchers made a demographic analysis of the area to show that parents and pupils reflected a lot of different opinions, and also, of course, a range of different living conditions. One could look upon this as a similar situation to the relations among the teachers. The problem was to do with trying to get teachers to use insights about community life to revise their existing impressions.

During the project it was possible to recognize differences in the way the teachers talked about parents. In some cases they even talked about different factions of parents divided into the same variables that we, in the beginning, introduced for separating factions among the teachers. But, of course, the main thing is that the teachers, in terms of their relationships with the community, have taken steps to analyse, instead of just relying on their impressions of the people living in the community.

Summing up our experience shows that in different fields it is possible for a group of teachers to adopt theories and methods from the co-operation between researchers themselves, and to transform them into useful tools in school life. And it looks as if the transformations are also useful after the researchers have left the scene.

References

Jensen, K. (1984). 'Analyse og intervention', in E. Henriksen, S. Hessel-holdt, K. Jensen and O. Larsen *Intervention og magt*. Copenhagen, Royal Danish School of Educational Studies, Pedagogy and Psychology Papers 30.

Jensen, K. (1986). 'Work, education and democratization', in S. Walker and L. Barton *Youth, Unemployment and Schooling*. Milton Keynes, Open University Press.

Larsen, O.B. (1986). *A Study of the Unified Danish 'Folkschool'*. Edited for Unesco, Copenhagen, Royal Danish School of Educational Studies.

Touraine, A. (1982). *The Voice and the Eye*. Cambridge, Cambridge University Press.

Vilmar, F. (1973). *Strategien der Demokratisierung*. Darmstadt, Luchterhand Verlag.

(ii) The Kinkerhoek project: inequalities of opportunity

Piet Deckers and Marja van Erp

1. Introduction

Since 1950 it has been possible to note a developing interest, both in The Netherlands and abroad, in the question of whether the educational chances available to children coming from what are known as disadvantaged backgrounds can be increased, by means of changes in the school system coupled with attempts to enrich their environment. Seen historically, this growing interest can be related to increased competitiveness throughout the world, to attempts to integrate marginal social groupings and to the rise of movements bent on improving democracy.

Interest in the inequality of educational opportunities for distinct social groupings – and, on a more general level, interest in social inequality – gained much of its force from a series of empirical studies in the 1960s and 1970s. Empirical study, moreover, preceded, accompanied and followed a great many projects for change. These studies clearly showed that children from disadvantaged backgrounds – children of the uneducated manual workers and an increasing number of children from ethnic minorities – are, even when they are of (more than) normal intelligence, poorly equipped to function successfully either at school or in society. These children run a considerable risk of becoming cultural and social outsiders through social circumstances for which they are not responsible.

We wish to explore the ideas behind a Dutch reaction to this interest. We shall give an outline of developments in Dutch national policy, followed by a detailed description of a major, and completed, project of educational innovation: the Amsterdam Innovation Project (AIP). (See Part One, Chapter 4 for an example of work in this project.) This has had a stimulating effect on national policy and is a source of experience which can be used to help think about and to develop other attempts at innovation.

2. Developments in national education policy

Until recently, the Dutch education system was characterized by:

(a) a sharp divide between 'infant' (4 to 6 years) and 'primary' (6 to 12 years) schooling: the first pupil-oriented, the second performance-oriented;

(b) a great commitment in the 'primary' school to a curriculum designed on traditional lines. Using textbooks in which teaching material is grouped along a linear increase in difficulty, the teaching material was worked through by practice and training in class;

(c) the isolated position of education in society;

(d) certain discrepancies in the aims and methods of the two ministries (Education and Science, and Welfare, Health and Cultural Affairs) concerned with education.

In 1973 a national policy aimed at the reorganization of education generally and at the stimulation of the education of pupils in disadvantaged situations was adopted. The overall innovation policy was designed to bring about a form of 'primary' school which would embrace the functions of the 'infant' and 'primary' schools within a single school for children aged from 4 to 12. The features of such a school have been formulated as follows: uninterrupted development of all pupils; attention to the pupil's individual identity; stimulation of creativity; improved diagnostic and remedial functioning of education; and the removal of the educational disadvantage suffered by children from socially deprived milieux.

This new 'primary' school for children aged from 4 to 12 was implemented on a national scale in 1985. A few years earlier, in 1982, the influence of parents and pupils on the contents of education and the organization of the learning process was regulated by law.

Parallel with the overal educational renewal policy, since 1974, there has been a special stimulation policy intended to give children from socio-economically deprived backgrounds the same educational chances as children in more favourable circumstances. This policy treats educational disadvantage as only one aspect of unfavourable social circumstances, and it is for this reason that measures have been taken for both an improvement in education and for changes in the areas of social welfare (through an attempt at improving relations between school, family and local environment). Changes have been made to the stimulation policy in the 1980s. Its scope was widened by replacing the concept of socio-economic disadvantage with the concept of educational disadvantage. As well as groups disadvantaged by socio-economic circumstances the policy now pays particular attention to ethnic minorities, children of parents who have no permanent address or who travel widely, and to girls. The second change has to do with the integration of the stimulation programme into the general renewal policy. In this connection, work was started in 1982 on the design of a so-called Education Priorities Plan in which statutory regulations will take the place of the previous *ad hoc* policy. Up until now this law has not been ratified by the Dutch Parliament.

3. The Amsterdam Innovation Project (AIP)

In 1971/2, under the inspired leadership of Dr Co van Calcar, a seven-year educational innovation project (AIP) started in Amsterdam. The intention was to minimize the educational problems experienced by children in older urban areas and to increase their opportunities for development. The immediate reason for setting up the AIP was the discovery that children in older parts of the city – largely the children of skilled and unskilled workers – were lagging behind other pupils in terms of educational achievement: their performance at 'primary' school was lower and fewer of them went on to higher forms of secondary education after leaving 'primary' school. Generally speaking, the opportunities for personal development that are open to pupils at 'primary' schools in The Netherlands are fitted to the needs of the middle class. Teaching has little to do with experience, often limiting itself to a number of areas of knowledge in which previously acquired skills are further developed through practice and training. For many children from older parts of the city, in contrast to those pupils wo do have sufficient extracurricular opportunities, this formal education had scarcely any meaning: neither the reason for learning nor the use of having learnt something had any connection with their world. They were merely subjected passively to an impersonal obligation to perform without reward.

The AIP therefore made the experiences and perceived world of these children the starting-point for education and integrated the traditional reading and practice material into this pattern. At the same time, the AIP initiated collaborative projects with local community centres, libraries and social groupings in order to improve the extra-curricular opportunities and activities open to these children and to broaden their horizons. In this way, a connection was created between school and the world beyond school. However, the changes advocated by the AIP were not confined to teaching. The AIP has also involved school, family and neighbourhood more closely with each other by the attunement of activities. This permitted the exploitation of experiences and the application of skills to take place in a wider arena. In this way, organizational conditions were created for a broadening of the social supporting structure through greater involvement of the local people.

4. Philosophy, objective and evaluation

Children in older districts of the city, most of whom are the children of low-paid workers, fare worse at school than their peers, even during the first year at school, and the gap gets worse as the years go by. Various theories have been put forward to explain this discrepancy. One suggests that compared with the middle classes and well-to-do, inner-city children have limited experiences, they suffer, in other words, from experience deprivation. Others would have it that their experiences are not inferior, but different. The AIP had a view of society in which everybody was in principle equal and it attacked the inequality which existed in practice from that point of view. The low-paid lack the material and cultural goods which make possible the diversity and multiplicity of experiences which is valued in education. Poverty of experience is a derived poverty. Where experiences are the same, language or cognitive growth will be the same. Thus, the children of the lower paid have fewer educational opportunities. Due to the social position of their parents, the experience they gain of life is less varied than or different from that gained by other children. And, because school has too few opportunities to offer them to make up for the missing experience, whilst at the same time its teaching activities have too little obvious relevance to the experience that children *do* have, their handicaps multiply.

The material and cultural reality experienced by the children of the low-paid is limited, and this demands more fundamental solutions than compensating programmes. The implication of this analysis for the organization of education is that it must first of all ensure a broadening of horizons and opportunities for development, so that the acquisition of technical skills is provided with a proper foundation. On the other hand, education will not become meaningful to pupils until it is made relevant to their own experiences. Elaborated in terms of its relevance for society, this analysis means that educational reality ought to be brought more directly under the control of the working classes by way of a just distribution of material and cultural wealth.

The above view of the relation between experience and reality has been, together with the proposed solutions, a source of antitheses within the AIP and outside it in established institutions and interests. In debate between the 'deficit hypothesis' and the 'difference hypothesis' the AIP adopted a unique position by developing the 'culture hypothesis' just formulated. It may be concluded from experience within the AIP that the cultural hypothesis has given evidence of its considerable utility value for the new approach to education.

The AIP set itself the following general objective: 'the development of means, procedures and structures in the main areas of influence on education and the environment, following the rules of action-research, so that it would become possible to bring about an enduring reduction in the educational problems of children from disadvantaged backgrounds'.

The AIP was the experimental component of a policy conceived for a longer term. For evaluation, a large number of research projects were carried out, all in the chosen form of action-research. One implication of this approach was that, in contrast with traditional designs, the research was embedded in the function of evaluating the processes of change that had been embarked upon. Project decisions were taken in joint consultation with various parties involved, taking the research data into consideration. In the philosophy of the AIP, evaluation is both crucial and a matter for all concerned. In this broad design for evaluation, it is assumed that researchers bring in their own insights and results but that they have no absolute claim to truth and validity. For a theoretical elaboration of this point of view three interlinked evaluation components are distinguished: system evaluation, goal evaluation and 'tone evaluation'.

In system evaluation attention is paid to the conditions regarded as necessary for a change of pupil behaviour in the direction of the stated objective. It is concerned with both means (such as theme books), procedures (thematic and formal curriculum-oriented teaching, rules for taking decisions) and structures (policy design and collaborative structures between institutions).

Goal evaluation is directed towards establishing changes in pupil behaviour with respect to both cognitive performance and skills, and in social and emotional development.

A uniquely new dimension was added to the evaluation with the introduction of the concept of 'tone evaluation'. In this, persons directly involved, such as parents, pupils and teachers, are given an opportunity to give their assessment of the reforming activities in their own words and against the background of their own 'thought frameworks'. With this in mind, for those who are unable to participate directly in the activities of the project, so-called school portraits were written, giving a systematic description of the changes in terms of everyday reality.

5. Participants, project structure and strategy

Directly involved in the AIP were: 'infant' and 'primary' schools in Amsterdam, the Educational Advice and Guidance Centre (Advies- en Begeleidingscentrum voor het Onderwijs – ABC) and the Education Research Centre at the University of Amsterdam (Stichting Centrum voor Onderwijsonderzoek – SCO). All the schools were in older districts and urban-renewal areas of the city and had a high percentage of children from working-class families.

They all subscribed to the aims of the AIP, though their assessments of proposed solutions to problems were often not unanimous, so that the innovation process started off with a large number of different detailed amendments. The following numbers of schools took part in the project:

(a) In the Old West district, of 29 'primary' schools with 3792 pupils (of whom 2411 were in state-run, 1381 in privately run schools), 14 were fully involved in the project and all the rest took some part; of 23 'infant' schools (with 662 children at state-run and 582 in private establishments), again 14 were fully involved and the others took some part.

(b) In the North, of 41 'primary' schools with 7220 pupils (4020 in state, 3200 in private schools), 19 were fully involved in the project and all the rest took some part; of 36 'infant' schools (with 928 children in state-run, 934 in privately run establishments), again 18 were fully involved and the others took some part.

(c) In the East, of 25 'primary' schools with 4036 pupils (2775 in state, 1261 in private schools), all were either fully or partially involved in the project; of 20 'infant' schools (with 836 children in state-run, 652 in privately run establishments), again all were involved in the project to some extent.

The ABC is the education advisory service for Amsterdam. Its chief objective is the democratization of education. It provides support for schools with individual or structural difficulties, working with decentralized and multidisciplinary teams in the districts: within the AIP it took responsibility for most of the guidance and advice given to schools, the development work and the field-work. The SCO is an educational research institute, part of the University of Amsterdam. The institute conducted the overall research for the AIP and was directly involved at a number of experimental schools.

The structure of the project can be described as large-scale, experimental (for a limited number of schools with simultaneous implementation and dissemination in a larger group of schools, changing in time as modifications became necessary), and diffuse in the starting-up period. The reforms started in 1971 in the bottom class of the 'primary' school and in the 'infant' school. After this, each school-year, the project shifted its attention one class higher. The project was extended to a larger number of schools and districts (North and East) in 1973, the new schools being able to profit from the experience gained in the first two years, taking over what they judged to be suitable solutions for their own particular problems. During the course of the project, the conclusion was arrived at that an overall strategy for change would offer more opportunities for success than an innovation strategy for each successive school year.

In elaborating the objectives at schools the AIP took the following as its starting-point. The improvement of educational opportunities for working–class children by means of reform of the content and organization of education, with, for the time being, no change to the usual standards applying to pupils' performance. This strategy was considered necessary to meet fears expressed by teachers and parents with respect to expectations relating to the level of achievement that conventional wisdom regards as necessary. It was successful in the sense that the AIP was perceived by parents and schools as having the quality of education at heart.

6. Elaboration of objectives in schools

By making the experiences of the pupils the starting–point for education the old education system was turned upside–down. If the teacher uses text books, she knows what subjects she has covered, that there is a progression in the teaching material and that she has fulfilled the stipulated teaching objectives if she gets to the end of the book on time. With the new reforms she lost this yardstick; worse still, she was not trained to let pupils take an active and independent role in the teaching process. With the help of an intensive pro-gramme of practice, during which teachers learned how to exploit the experiences of pupils, and by a strategy aimed at those concerns teachers had about pupil performance levels – which pointed the way for changes of course and proved a major determinant in the motivation of the teachers themselves – teaching in Amsterdam was changed in the desired direction without sacrificing the positive aspects of the traditional approach. Let us now look at how these changes were carried through. By way of illustration, emphasis will be laid on the area of language teaching.

We distinguish three different steps which were and had to be taken. As a first step some so–called 'theme books' were developed to introduce the changes to the 'infant' schools and the first two classes of the 'primary' schools. These books gave teachers a concrete example of how the usual learning objectives could be combined with a new teaching approach. Features of the books were:

1. pupils' experiences and their perceived world, summarized to make up important themes, as the starting-point for teaching,

2. the concept of communication as a major new purpose of education, and,
3. a progression through the series from the close-to-home and the everyday to the far-away and the unknown.

Pupils' horizons were extended by exploring the neighbourhood and by excursions beyond it. In particular, the creative assimilation of experiences, taking the form of discussion in class, book compilation by pupils, letter-writing and so on made a positive contribution towards breaking through the old method of formal teaching.

As a second step a number of 'primary' and 'infant' schools decided that the chief focus of attention should be on collaboration, the starting-points being the realization of continuous, individual opportunities for development for pupils aged between 4 and 8 and the extension of and differentiation in what schools had to offer by way of experience. Both of these starting-points proved capable of being put into practice: in some 'primary' schools the organization of and approach to education practised in infant schools has become firmly established. To achieve this, both classrooms and other areas such as corridors and the assembly hall have been given over to some extent to 'experience centres' along the lines of those in some British and American schools. These centres contain a quantity of material about a particular subject or theme (for example, there might be a counting centre, a cooking centre, a biology centre, and so on). Depending on their interests and needs the pupils can work in a wide variety of centres either individually or in groups.

The combination of traditional learning goals and themes, conceived in the lower school as thematic syllabuses, was projected on into the upper school in the form of learning-through-projects. In designing projects (e.g. to study living conditions, occupations, or the division of roles between the sexes), two problems became apparent. In the first place, it became clear that there was a lack of information sources in schools. At the same time, it was difficult for pupils to classify the information brought in in a systematic manner. This argued for more attention to documentary centres and skills. The second problem proved somewhat intractable. With the decision to take actuality, experiences, or interests as the starting-point for teaching, the safe path of the textbooks was abandoned and the teacher now felt herself to be responsible for the adequate treatment, assimilation and practising of the formal learning goals. Providing exercise material on specific problems demanded a knowledge of the essentials of the matter, now that the set teaching method was no longer being followed. And at the same time, precisely because the method had been abandoned, it was unclear whether the formal aspect of the subject had been covered with sufficient thoroughness. To help the teacher to find exercise material and to monitor pupil performance in comparison with traditional schooling, the existing language textbooks and project descriptions were inventoried and classified, as the third step. All objectives of thematic teaching were placed under one heading (using language) and all formal curriculum objectives under a second (thinking about language). With this aid it was found possible to look for practice material for the two areas and for the teacher to keep track of what had been done with regard to language activities. Because all the objectives of language teaching were now shown together in a single scheme, the teacher was given a stimulus for making a conscious choice between particular goals.

With this inventory and classification, an instrument had been created for the realization of reform in which a decline in the traditional standard of performance would not automatically follow. In practice, this instrument has not been used to the full. It frequently proved too complex and gave inadequate practical guidance in the matter of new learning objectives.[1] The problem of monitoring pupil performance levels remained: there was no practical means of keeping track of the material already dealt with and the material still to be treated. It proved no simple matter to change the use of teaching textbooks. These are the steps we took in the AIP. After 1978, the ABC and the schools developed things further. The need for further development was triggered off by the influx of large groups of children from ethnic minorities into the schools.

7. School, family and local environment

Schools (alone) cannot bring about an enduring lessening of inequality of opportunity, simply because inequality is a social fact. As the first step towards forging better links between school and society, the AIP campaigned for closer collaboration between (and mutual attunement of) school, family and local environment. At the micro level this attunement was given shape in the theme books, the experience centre and project teaching. At the macro level arguments were put forward for measures to be taken on a municipal and national scale.

To improve relations between school, family and local environment a number of activities were developed. These were known collectively as field-work, and included both the work undertaken by the school to explore the neighbourhood and the living conditions of its pupils, and the activities of the field-workers, parents and local organizations to improve the living environment for themselves.

As regards school and family field-work, the following was done. Teaching was attuned to life in and outside the home by visiting families, exploring the neighbourhood, and getting pupils to talk about their experiences. Parents gained an insight into what the school and their children were doing from a school newspaper, parent–teacher meetings and pupil discussions. Schools were opened up for parental access at any time and for parental help at school. As far as possible the AIP has involved parents in changes in schools and has been active in promoting democratic decision-making. Using what was referred to as an informative parent questionnaire, parents were kept informed about changes and asked for their opinions. Decisions on whether or not changes should go ahead were taken at parent–teacher meetings. In this way parental fears of a loss of traditional quality of education and other concerns were converted into participation.

Furthermore, the following initiatives were important:

- toy and playground projects in which parents and community organizations jointly campaigned for the improvement of play facilities for children;
- annual information markets for parents and pupils on different types of secondary education;
- homework classes for secondary school pupils on different types of secondary education;
- regularization of working contacts between educational and neighbourhood services so that increased opportunities for personal development and improvement of the living environment could be the targets of joint action from community and youth centres, libraries and a variety of working parties;
- reinforcement and intensification of contacts between parents, teachers and other professional workers, with a view to a satisfactory mutual attunement of living conditions, educational situations and schooling and training activities;
- reinforcement and extension of the means of expression available to all involved. A striking example of this is the so-called 'language printing shop' (*Taaldrukwerkplaats*). This is a sort of printing shop where children and adults can set their own experiences, wishes and campaign needs for active distribution in print. The language printing shops are generally the scene of

intensive teamwork between schools, local institutions, action groups and such bodies as the libraries and 'creativity centres'.

8. Results

The results of the AIP have been described in a large number of interim and specialist reports, recorded on film, collected together in a three-part summarizing report and subjected to critical assessment in a number of external evaluation initiatives. At the level of the system the following results can be noted.

1. Fundamental changes were noted at the level of concrete teaching practice as regards teacher attitudes to pupils, the interaction between pupils, and the content of the teaching material used.
2. Thematic teaching is possible without neglecting the traditional learning objectives.
3. For the teacher, a combination of thematic and traditional learning goals proves to be difficult in its practical elaboration. It is not easy to leave the safety of textbooks. A continuous discussion is necessary about the essential goals and ways to reach them. The 'experience centres' and 'documentation centres' proved to be a success.
4. Despite initial scepticism and numerous problems of habituation at the start of the project, collaboration between schools and external bodies proved feasible in an atmosphere of mutual understanding at the practical level. Any obstacles in this area were generally found to exist at the policy level, a fact that, to some extent, can be explained by a difference in administrative premises and working principles in the two ministries concerned, the resultant separate administrative orders, rules and conditions for financing, and the various disciplines falling under their control.
5. The AIP had a decisive influence on teachers and schools in Amsterdam. In 1988 there are still schools who call themselves 'AIP schools'. These schools and the ABC played an important role in the dissemination and further development of AIP objectives, means and procedures.
6. On the basis of the results from the final evaluation the city authorities, taking the AIP approach as their guideline, have confirmed and stepped up their support for positive discrimination by means of a revised policy framework. The new policy framework also pays special attention to new developments

relating *inter alia* to the ethnic minorities and secondary schooling. Nevertheless, the sharp decline in the economic situation
currently poses a serious political impediment to the implementation of idea of positive discrimination in favour of disadvantaged groups. One thing that *is* certain is that, in view of
the changed circumstances, new demands will be made on
inventiveness and creative thinking in order to find workable
expedients.

7. The premisses and acquired insights of thematic teaching were
   included for further elaboration in the activities of the national
   curriculum institute (Stichting voor de Leerplanontwikkeling –
   SLO).

At the level of pupil behaviour we note the following results.

8. An improvement was noted in cognitive performance in the
   lower grades of the new 'primary' school.
9. In the upper grades there was no noticeable improvement in
   learning performance in the traditional areas of learning. In
   some respects, indeed, there was a slight decline. It should be
   noted, in explanation of this, that there were sharp fluctuations
   in the pupil composition of the schools in the older parts of the
   city due to renovation activities and the high influx of children
   from ethnic minorities in the 1970s.
10. Despite a multiplicity of changes the socio-emotional climate of
    the schools proved not to have been adversely affected. On some
    points, indeed, there was a noticeable improvement. For in-
    stance: a sociometric questionnaire showed an improvement of
    the relations between pupils over the years.

Regarding the concept of 'tone evaluation':

11. Parents were involved in the evaluation of AIP activities in a
    number of schools. In the first years of the AIP they generally
    approved of the innovations; in later years they approved, but at
    the same time became more critical. Reasons for this develop-
    ment could be either a greater concern for traditional learning
    goals as secondary education comes nearer, or a better insight
    into the consequences of innovations based on experience.

Since the end of the Innovation Project a lively debate has started
in various quarters concerning the value of the project model and the
significance of the insights gained through the project. Sometimes
the balance is in favour, sometimes against. What is certain is that the
debate will not be brought to an early conclusion.

(iii) Villeneuve College: managing permanent innovations

Jean Berbaum

It has been found that in a good many school innovations, procedures which are out of the ordinary last only as long as the presence in the institution of the teacher or administrator who instigated them. An inventive pedagogical idea only exceptionally outlives its creator. Therefore, I wish to gather here a few considerations on the conditions which give the possibility of a certain permanency of the innovative features in a specific school institution. For this purpose, I shall base my argument mainly on the example of the experimental secondary school of La Villeneuve, in Grenoble (see Part 1, Chapter 4). In the first part I shall try to characterize the innovations currently being attempted. In the second part I shall analyse the reasons for their vulnerability and the conditions for permanency of these innovations.

Let's say, for the sake of clarity, that we can call an innovation any pedagogical practice, any organization that introduces a change, a shift from traditional forms of teaching. The origin of innovations is most often the fact that new dimensions in the teaching situation are taken into account, to diversify the ways of the practice of teaching. And the question that arises is, of course, to know the extent to which an innovation can be other than temporary, provisional, closely linked to a particular event. Isn't it in the very nature of innovation to be constantly put into question? Can we assume that what has been devised by a teacher in relation to a particular situation he has encountered, could be generalized? Wouldn't that mean, in some ways, the denial of innovation? It's because we think that there are certainly some sides of innovation that merit a certain permanency that we consider it important to reflect on the conditions of that permanency as a means of developing the educational system.

If one tries to classify innovations, one can first set them out according to their origin. Taking the example of Villeneuve, one would first have to mention the existence of a 'charter', an agreement, which has inspired most of the innovations decided upon since 1972. Between the council authorities and the representatives of national education, an agreement was signed on the experimental secondary school, which commissioned the institution to pay special attention to the prevention of both school failure and any form of social segregation, as well as to open itself to the 'environment'. The specificity of the experimental school lies in assigned co-operative time included in the teacher's schedule.

Innovations can also be, and not only in Villeneuve, the result of official decisions or orientations planned by the Ministry of Education. For instance, an Act established a schedule according to which ten per cent of the timetable could be left to the initiative of teachers and pupils. Other Acts have established programmes of remedial work, the provision of special time to pupils in remedial classes, group tutoring and homework training. Projects of educational action (PAE) are quite common at the moment in French schools, thanks to the fact that they have been officially authorized and enacted.

Some innovations can also be instigated by periodic proposals of contracts from the Ministry of Education, which give schools the opportunity to make their own suggestions for organizing research or specific teacher-training actions, which are then submitted for the authorities' agreement.

External support can also be found with research organizations such as the National Institute of Pedagogical Research (NIPR) which in Villeneuve (to take one example) provides an incentive for reflection and practical research on experiment and argument in the field of sciences. The regional scheme of teacher-training also provides, through the training courses set up, a further source of encouragement for the launching of new forms of pedagogical actions. There too, we can point out, for instance, the work undertaken in school libraries' documentary departments on the use of visual aids, files and records. We can recall the work done in the field of evaluation, and on methodological help to learners.

As well as the innovations set up by ministerial initiatives, research institutions, or teacher-training organizations, one ought to mention, of course, the innovations which proceed from collective or individual initiatives. For instance, an example can be found in the prolongation of the 1972 charter, which allows for the integration of the lower-ability pupils into the secondary school, instead of segregating them. Then, still keeping to the example of Villeneuve, it is of extreme importance to emphasize the running of the school in six 'houses' or mini-schools, co-ordinated with each other but each dealing independently with timetables and teachers' co-operative work. Among individual initiatives we could note a good many efforts for a better knowledge of the pupils, of their learning processes, for methodological help in general, or for the development of a different way of teaching. We can mention here the case of the teaching of English as a foreign language, which is reported elsewhere in this volume (pp. 63–7).

These are merely some examples, not a full inventory of the achievements reported from Villeneuve, and from other schools of the region. We can notice that innovations may have varied origins, but we must not ignore the fact that, in the French school system, initiatives which are not based directly on a written act, or an official organization, always require approval from the authorities. Heads and school inspectors are necessarily referred to, in order to approve the undertaking of any innovation.

The above innovations presented in relation to their institutional, individual, or collective origin, could also be classified according to the changes they bring about. We might then distinguish between innovations leading to changes in school structure, in teaching practice, or in teachers' attitudes. In that way, the launching of the mini-school organization or the setting up of out-of-school practical sessions which lead the school to establish agreements with firms, bring about many modifications in structure. They may be decided on by the teachers, but these innovations bring about changes which are recorded in official documents to which others are then able to refer, and this guarantees a certain permanency.

This guarantee does not exist when the innovation is linked to a change in teaching practice, which often depends on an individual teacher's goodwill or initiative. Though official approval might be a necessary condition, it is by no means a sufficient condition. The introduction of a reorganization in sessions or full days devoted to the same subject, cannot be done through mere authority. The teachers involved must agree with it, and although authorities may wish such changes, they can't impose them. Of course, the same thing happens with innovations which are due to changes of attitude: modifying one's behaviour towards pupils or parents can't be imposed by rules. Yet this is a significant dimension of the renewal of secondary schools, and is given special attention in Villeneuve. One understands, then, how any innovation which corresponds to a change in attitude will be vulnerable.

It is, therefore, at the same time both a decision by the authorities at their different levels, regional and local, *and* an approval from the teachers concerned, which are necessary for an innovation to occur and to last. We mentioned the difficulties which may arise from both parties, and we must add those which arise from environment. An innovation very often bothers colleagues or trade unions or parents, even when all precautions have been taken, all the more if one has not given sufficient attention to informing people. The traditional practice of limited involvement on the part of the teacher, is likely to reappear at the least obstacle.

If this be so, if innovations are as fragile as we have just pictured them, one may ask what are the necessary circumstances for non-traditional practice to gain more permanency, more strength. There too, the example of Villeneuve and some of the remarks which have just been made, are going to be useful. We first have to recall the part played by all that is linked to the structure and the institution; a charter, agreements with external organizations like research institutes, as well as agreements with firms, that enable pupils to attend practical courses, certainly provide contributions to the permanence of innovations. The launching of projects (PAE) over a limited time, contracts for particular research-work, encourage perseverance in the action undertaken. As long as innovation concerns a group, and not only an individual, there is a further mutual support which can develop and play an important part in the continuity of the action. At the teachers' level as well as the pupils', the interest shown by an external observer, his theoretical support, the stimulation of a collective reflection, are further positive aspects of an action, which go beyond the minimum we may expect from a teacher. This kind of influence can be achieved by a researcher concerned with the work going on in a particular school. He has time to think out and to develop new ideas which will support innovations already introduced by the teachers. In doing this he helps the teacher to be conscious of the importance of his enterprise and he also brings the necessary adjuncts concerning both the content and the organization of the teaching. The researcher helps the teacher to find better arguments for answering criticisms which are inevitably voiced when someone does something which introduces change to the daily routine. What at last involves the actors of innovations is indirectly the publicity they may be led to make about their work. From the moment one draws attention to oneself, one feels responsible towards one's environment. One wishes not to disappoint. When a good image of a school has developed, it is difficult not to honour it, not to confirm it, through achievements.

If it is true that innovations are always vulnerable, that they depend at the same time on the goodwill of the different administrative authorities and on the interest shown by the teachers, it is none the less also true that they bring a renewed interest in their profession to those who undertake them. One may object that interest comes first and not the undertaken innovation. But whatever the object of innovation, modification of innovation will not be effective unless it takes on a certain permanency. We must give special care to that permanency to make the evolution of the teaching system itself possible.

Note

The AIP attached considerable importance to the introduction of new learning objectives, which were known as 'broader skills'. This term covers those skills that are useful for forming opinions, adopting attitudes and making decisions whether independently or together with others. The preconditions for this are that the individual can engage in discussion, listen, gather information, get a grasp of circumstances, and so on.

CHAPTER 9

Managing and monitoring democratization policy

School management and democratic education

Maria do Carmo Climaco

Introduction

The current Portuguese school management system was introduced in 1974, following the April Revolution. As is declared in the Bill that created it, the new democratic school management system should be both an ideal of a democratic society, and, simultaneously, a strategy to build such a society.

As a matter of fact, all governments since then have continuously been concerned with school management issues, either for political or pedagogical reasons. Schools reflect and strengthen the values, attitudes and relationships which exist in other sectors of society and they also act, or can act, as fundamental factors of change, by promoting the emergence of new experiences, attitudes and behaviour. Schools became more complex and mirrored all the conflicts of the new power relationships. Democratic authority had to be discovered, understood and accepted.

The changes occurring in Portuguese society in general created the need to promote equal opportunities of schooling for all children and youngsters. However, the strategies to implement new policy were not followed by meaningful changes in attitudes and practices within schools themselves, changes required to make equal opportunities of success for all possible. There was an expansion of the school welfare policy; new campaigns of adult education and basic literacy were undertaken; new schools were created; but, the cultural inheritance, specifically that with popular roots, was differently valued in contrast with the heroes and myths that had fed the chauvinism of the ancient, pre-1974, regime.

However, the traditional image of the authority of the school and its agents was progressively lost and questioned; new power relationships were established, as these developed in the larger society. New school competences were emphasized; some vague ideas here and there of 'deschooling the school' were preached; but, an evident contradiction, the selective function of the school went on and continued using the traditional norms for the evaluation of pupils – intellectual and academic knowledge.

Schools in Portugal had been too stable for too long. Stable in the kind of students they served – regarding their social and cultural background, their skills and behaviours. Stable in their teaching force – with respect to their social areas of recruitment, their professional qualifications and their belief system. Stable in their teaching and learning needs. And stable in the curricula, material and methods adopted for generation after generation. Teachers were not prepared to face the 'learning difficulties' of the socially disadvantaged children, and they literally did not know how to select appropriate teaching/learning strategies that might enhance the social, affective and cognitive development of these children. And this lack of understanding, together with lack of skill, contributed to the failure of a 'democratic dream' not rooted in the Portuguese reality. So democracy came to mean easier access to schooling for a larger stratum of the population; but it also meant a negative discrimination against these new arrivals, these new pupils who were different in origin and skills.

If the first Bills reinforced the concern for *democracy* and *democratic schooling*, after a period in schools of 'revolutionary enthusiasm', *'efficiency'* was a word that paralleled this concern in importance and frequency, as a consequence of the reforms themselves. Thus, the school democratization movement did manage to achieve easier access to school for larger sectors of the population, partly as a result of the general economic growth and of the facilitation of schooling through a new school welfare policy (including food, transportation, lodging and learning materials). On the other hand, there was a general demand for schooling to give expression to the common belief that education means more opportunities for social development and promotion. As a consequence, new schools were created and a large number of others became overcrowded, especially in the urban areas, where some buildings are still working in double-shift or even in three shifts. We could say that 25 to 40 per cent of them are overcrowded or heavily overcrowded (see Table 9.1).

Table 9.1   School population and space

	Less than normal population	*Normal population*	*Overcrowded*	*Heavily overcrowded*
Lower-junior Schools	20%	54%	21%	5%
Junior Schools	30%	41%	19%	10%
High Schools	16%	40%	34%	10%

Note: Most of the secondary schools have more than 1,000 students. Some have more than 3,000 students.

Corresponding to the increasing number of students in school there was an increasing demand for teachers for all subjects. For many university-leavers teaching became an alternative to unemployment. For schools, the demand created a need to design a new strategy to train the newcomers to the profession (see Table 9.2).

Table 9.2   Staff quality

	Trained staff	*Non-trained staff*
Lower-Junior School	53.3%	46.7%
Junior School	43.2%	56.8%
High School	49.4%	50.6%

Note: All primary teachers receive professional training.

In some curriculum areas, especially in some regions of the country, teachers were not academically fully qualified, but the alternative was to have no teachers at all. So, new in-service training programmes were established for all secondary teachers – from lower-junior to high schools – to prepare them scientifically and pedagogically, trying to achieve a balance between the former curriculum-centred programmes and the new school-centred ones. The aim was to develop schools as true educational environments, fully involving teachers, students and families.

New curricula were designed for primary and secondary schools, introducing new organizational patterns of studies and new curriculum areas aimed at the development of new attitudes and opportunities for development. Examples occurred at all levels: at primary school – 6 to 9 years – the system of four classes was substituted by a two-phase system as a means of reducing failure, by respecting the stages of children's development. The two-track system starting at 12 was postponed to the end of secondary education – 16 years – and vocational components in the curricula, education for working life and citizenship were introduced for all. A new system and criteria for students' assessment and evaluation was established as a natural consequence of these new attitudes towards education and schooling.

School management

In a context of change, the new school management system became a strategy to facilitate and reinforce democracy at school. Democracy implied participation, and, for change to be effective it was felt that teachers and students should be involved in the process of change and that appropriate structures of participation had to be created.

There are two distinct models of school management which have emerged, corresponding to two different realities: primary and secondary schools. Both have in common the direct participation of staff in the choice of their school leaders, through election.

The structures

In primary schools the *teachers' council* is made up of all the teachers in each school, on the organic structure responsible for the school management. This council elects the *director*. The smaller schools (one or two teachers) will join their nearest neighbour to form a unique council, which cannot be smaller than three teachers. The teachers' council is responsible for the pedagogical life of school, as well as for school welfare. The director is a co-ordinator and is responsible for administrative tasks. She/he is a teacher and only in schools larger than 16 teachers can she be freed from teaching duties. Administratively primary schools depend upon *municipal school delegacies*, which co-ordinate *all* primary schools in specific areas.

As can be seen in Figure 9.1, municipal school delegacies are at the heart of school management. In spite of them being only a ring in the long administrative chain, they are the first critical point where important decisions can be made. In each delegacy there is a person who is appointed by the central authorities, for periods of three years each. Pedagogically, schools link directly with central services. There are regional intermediate services to support the teachers' continuous training, special educational needs, artistic education, and methodology in general.

The characteristics of the schools' network constitute one of the main problems in the management of primary schools. Half of the total (10,000) are isolated and have no more than one or two teachers (see Table 9.3).

Only 30 per cent of schools have enough students to constitute four classes (one teacher per class) and 7 per cent of the schools have less than ten students. This, in itself, can explain the persistent teacher turnover. Isolation and hard living conditions are discouraging and don't promote development. This means that as soon as they

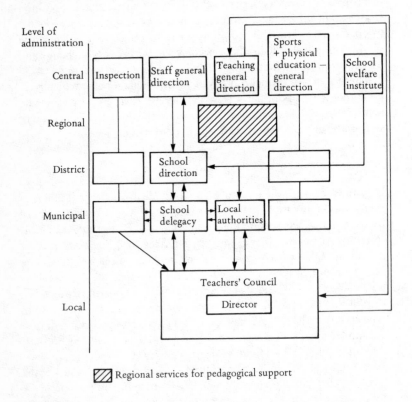

Regional services for pedagogical support

Figure 9.1　Primary school management system

Table 9.3   Primary school network

Teachers	1	2	3–6	7–11	12–16	16
%	28.5	25.5	31.2	8.4	3.2	2.1
		54.0				

can, teachers apply for a better place (a less isolated one) and leave the 'worse ones' for the younger teachers. But, when their 'turn' comes to be placed in an urban area, most teachers have lost important professional skills and their capacity for change or innovation.

At secondary school level, the management system has a different organization: schools depend hierarchically and functionally upon central services. Within schools, there are three management structures: the directive board, the pedagogical board and the administrative board (see Figure 9.3).

The Directive Board is constituted by 3 to 5 teachers (depending on the number of students: more or less than 1,000), one member from the non-teaching staff and one student from class delegates (in high schools only). All these members are elected by their peers. Teacher members choose the president from amongst themselves.

The Pedagogical Board is constituted by representatives from the different organizational groups in the school: the president of the directive board, who presides, curriculum area delegates, the tutors' co-ordinator, one student from each year and course (in high schools only), the teacher trainer (if there is one), and a representative from the Consulting Council. This council was recently created and is constituted by representatives from parents' association, local council authorities, cultural associations, students' association, and other people working at school (doctor, social worker, psychologist). It has been variously implemented, according to local traditions of participation. In many places it doesn't work at all. But it can

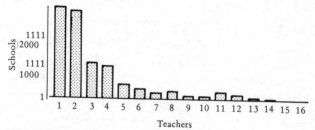

Figure 9.2   Number of primary teachers per school

constitute a meaningful attempt to develop the idea of social partnership for education at local level.

The Administrative Board is constituted by the president and the secretary of the directive board (who is in charge of school welfare) and the chief of the school administrative services.

The Pedagogical Board is responsible for the definition of the school educational policy, for the organization of teachers' continuing education and for the relationships between school and family, or school and community. There are other organizational structures at school level, namely the parents' association and the students' association. Though the elected directive board has been considered the *symbol* of our democratic management system, in fact, the pedagogical board is the point in the structure where the level of participation of teachers and students in school life can be best expressed and can best guarantee democratic life at the level of the school.

Democracy and efficiency

However, the reality in each school is diverse and sometimes 'democracy', in spite of its many faces, has little chance of survival.

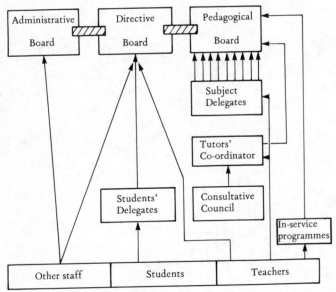

Figure 9.3 Secondary school management system

To foster it, it was considered important (a) to know how far this model has been implemented, (b) what managerial styles have been developed, (c) what constraints have been affecting school efficiency, (d) what knowledge we can produce from our experience, and (e) how we can use management as an effective strategy of change and development.

In this spirit, the Studies and Planning Bureau of the Ministry of Education developed a three-year project, designed to identify (a) which indicators should be used to assess the model and the practice of school management; (b) which critical factors in the system or in the model hindered or fostered the development of democratic life at school; (c) which strategies might be proposed to guarantee the quality of school life and education. The study was conducted at national level, using questionnaires and interviews addressed to a meaningful sample of schools and teachers. On the basis of existing literature, we used, among others, some indicators related to the number of elected directive boards, the turnover rate in the management boards, the level of participation in the decision-making process, and the level of difficulties and satisfaction with managerial functions.

Some results

In only 50 per cent of schools is the directive board elected. In the other cases teachers choose three teachers whose names are presented to the central administration. One of them is nominated president, who chooses his/her own team. This team will run the school for a single year, instead of a normal two-year period. However, very often, after that first year, they agree to be re-elected for a further couple of years or even more, as is shown in Table 9.4.

School managers have no specific training and so it is necessary to take advantage of their experience. There is no management career and it has been assumed that anyone who is a good teacher will also be a good manager. If in primary schools this assumption can be

Table 9.4 Management experience

Lower Junior Schools		High Schools	
1st Mandate	2nd and higher Mandate	1st Mandate	2nd and higher Mandate
31.2%	44.6%	28.5%	59.4%

more easily accepted, the complexity, the scale and the organiz-ational demands of secondary schools made it clear that these functions correspond to different competences. More and more teachers demand specific training in school management, beyond the general information included in the professional training of any teacher. The lack of training, especially in administrative issues, is one of the critical factors that has contributed for the shortage of 'volunteers' for managerial functions. Teachers indicated the following as factors of great difficulty in school management:

- a shortage of budgets
- a lack of autonomy in the management of the budget
- a shortage of room and/or bad conditions of buildings
- a lack of support
- individualism of teachers
- the handling of personal conflicts.

However, they recognize that through management they can be more responsible for life in school, and have more opportunities (to form a team and share responsibilities and to diversify their tasks, to have no hierarchical dependencies and be autonomous). And all these aspects appear to be sources of personal satisfaction.

In the same way, pedagogical boards have similar difficulties in finding teachers to accept election as a delegate, especially in secondary schools.

If we analyse the decision-making process in different aspects of school life, 'power' belongs to the *directive board*, even in the peda-gogical domain. Frequently, the pedagogical board acts as an assembly of school representatives, whose span of intervention depends upon the management style of the directive board, on their leadership skills, on their presentations of school life and their role, of their own skill, and so on.

The autonomy of schools, then, is weak. Even where the law expressly states that it is within the pedagogical board's competence to define criteria for the constitution of classes, for the organization of space and time, for the distribution of teachers' work-load; to manage the curricula; to implement extra-curricular activities, and so on – it is only half realized. As a matter of fact, there are strict 'knowns' about school organization, and recommendations (or suggestions) on curriculum development, on how to use materials, on teaching methods, and so on. But it is always possible to narrow or to enlarge the degree of autonomy and to make structures work or not.

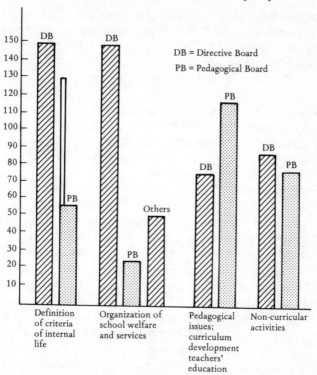

Figure 9.4 Participation in the decision-making process

However, there are external factors related to the general management of the system that affect the efficiency of schools and work against any innovation. One of the more frequently referred to is the national system of teachers' recruitment and staff allocation. A large percentage of teachers do not work in the places they would prefer, or where they live. This reduces their capacity of participation and intervention in school life and explains high turnover rates and absenteeism. In small schools more than half of the teachers move every year, and in extreme cases, from a total staff of 16 or 40, only one or two of them will stay at their school.

Participation and efficiency

The structures of participation are important devices designed to promote the democratization of school and education. However, democratization of schooling is not a goal in itself, but a strategy to promote personal and social development. The same organizational structures can be used both to *foster* and to *hinder* participation in the decision-making process, in the name of school efficiency. Participation is not an obvious experience and has to be learnt. The best way to learn it is by participating: participating in the access to and production of information about school and education, in the sharing of responsibilities, in creating conditions of participation. Underlying the structures – elected or nominated – we can find different organizational ideologies that reflect the teachers' educational ideas and perceptions, their values, their personal and professional developments. This is what really counts in making schools different.

Some schools could be described as curriculum-centred. Teachers' and students' participation is low and all innovation is introduced from the top down. School does not serve; school is served. The management style is formal, efficient and favours a bureaucratic and centralized administration. What matters is the observation of all norms and rules. All conduct tends to reduce the already limited field of autonomy left for schools.

Some other schools are teacher-centred ones. Generally these are very dynamic schools, full of initiatives and innovation. Frequently they correspond to teacher-training centres: the major concern in these is to create conditions which favour the teachers' work: space, time and equipment are provided in line with teaching needs. Management teams favour a humanistic relationship amongst staff and reinforce co-operative behaviour amongst teachers. Students do have to conform to teachers' plans and curriculum objectives, and their participation is very reduced. Teachers will participate for their own sake.

In student-centred institutions, the school is organized and responds to students' needs and aims to promote student participation in different aspects of school life, as a process of education. Emphasis is given to processes, not to contents.

It is impossible to conceive of school as an educational context separating students' development or education from the teachers' own development or education. The process is an interactive and pro-active one, which means that development is a result of mutual influences and that it can be a goal and a motivation in itself. One of the roles of a democratic school management system is to make that integrated development possible. Then there will be efficient schools as well as democratic ones.

CHAPTER 10

Democratization on trial

Democratization in English secondary schools

Colin Fletcher

Introduction

My father was a draughtsman who later became a teacher. My mother was a bank clerk until marriage. They talked about schools. He said that discipline should be self-discipline, teachers should show the effort needed to do a job well. He thought sensitivity should be in everybody's head, heart and hands. Good teaching was hard, he said, you show how you would do something and have to be constructive when the learner makes mistakes. My mother wanted her children to be as happy and successful as natural abilities allowed. My parents' views fitted each other, father on the features of good teaching and mother on its functions. In our house good teaching came from a love of the subject and its usefulness, put together with a respect for the learner and their prospects.

Meanwhile, I loathed grammar school and its contrasts with my parents' idealism. They were open and optimistic, my school was mostly fearful and cynical. I left never wanting to have anything to do with schools again.

I studied social sciences at university and then specialized in organizational research. At the same time, through direct struggles, I was learning about community power. Then, years later, I got the job of a lifetime, employed by a university Adult Education

Department with a five-year contract to record and help the development of a new community education centre.

A mixed comprehensive school was the major partner in the centre. I was guarded about the school and followed what was happening like a hunter. But the school was as my parents had hoped – and more. I felt pushed from mistrust onto a fence of scepticism and then over into the work to make the school experience worthwhile for everyone. I came to realize that this school was advocating an education in democracy and an education for democracy.

A few schools have openly advocated democracy, more have projected ambiguity and so protected themselves. 'Advocacy schools' tell us most about what democratic comprehensives are and how they come about. Their subsequent trials also tell us how 'ambiguous schools' avoid being stopped in making their more limited progress. The hostility which 'advocacy schools' have received, then suppression or severe set-backs are part of the reason for ambiguity. A further part is that 'advocacy schools' express the purpose of empowerment whilst 'ambiguity schools' put forward a mix of efficiency and enrichment as their purpose.

There are 'antagonistic' schools too, schools which are hostile to any purposes or practices which are not those of business efficiency.

I saw the struggle over an advocacy democratic comprehensive. With two friends I researched what happened and then we studied three similar but earlier trials (Fletcher *et al.* 1985). These schools were taking two related risks. They were extending the rights of their participants and they were attracting the attention of those who wanted to remove or restrict such rights. First, I want to outline what democratic comprehensives are and how they can be explained, at least in England, of course. Secondly, I want to describe the main features of their trials to show what ambiguously democratic comprehensives quite rightly fear.

Being a democratic comprehensive

'What does this term, "democratic comprehensive", mean as far as the participants are concerned?' (Fletcher *et al.* 1985, p. 136).

For pupils

- Elections within teaching groups for their representatives to a school council.
- School council meetings and teaching groups' discussions during teaching time.

- The right of the school council to complain, to criticize and to propose.
- The school council sets the students' standard of dress and appearance.

For teachers

- Members of a team in a shared area.
- Staff meetings at which they can determine the agenda, the extent of discussion, and the significance of voting.
- Working parties on developments.
- Participation in staff selection.

For headteacher

- 'Charismatic' in expressions of confidence in the ability of staff and pupils; emphasizes principles rather than details.
- Non-bureaucratic with a low emphasis on paperwork and a commitment to its open and full circulation.
- Leadership responsibilities largely in relation to the world outside, tirelessly 'explaining' the school.

For parents

- Regarded as partners.
- Right of open access.
- Opportunities for parent education and as parent helpers.
- Elections of parent governors.

For governing body

- All parties – parents, teachers, pupils, politicians – have their own elected representatives.
- There is a balance of interests such that no single group holds an effective majority.

These characteristics emphasize formal roles and meetings and 'the most important single proposition is that the democratic school brings together a redefinition of the roles of all its participants in the hope of greater identification and trust from one to another' (Fletcher *et al.* 1985, p. 139). But structure is no good without culture. Therefore:

The democratic comprehensive is more than committed ideals and idealists on committees. First and foremost it is recognizable through the democracy of everyday life, through curriculum choices for staff and pupils, through first name terms, through comfortable dress and through the messages on its walls and windows. Choices within the curriculum and in appearance and the ease of social relationships are all aspects of democracy in learning.

Democratic issues occur in curriculum choices too; such as environmental studies, personal relationships and citizenship. The school is more comprehensive because it openly explores the tension points within the development of democratic society. Issues of race and gender, for example, become foci of learning. As problems and potentials are perceived in adult life they become projects in school life. (Fletcher *et al.* 1985, pp. 139–40, adapted).

A democratic comprehensive refuses to do a number of things. First, it refuses to accept that the big conflict over schools is whether to educate wealth producers or worldly-wise people. The conflict is not between an economic purpose and a social purpose. The deeper conflict is between these two forms of adjustment to what is happening in society and a critical, political attitude towards whether it is good or bad, can be shifted or stopped. In democratic comprehensives, a political attitude is not deferred, it is developed. In many respects, the school tackles adult issues and political forms within an atmosphere and working relationships which are more like those of a positive primary school. In making a bridge from primary school to adult life, the school is less devoted to controlling adolescence. Its teachers argue that there are much more serious problems to be faced than the inevitable freedom-fighting of teenagers.

There are three ways of explaining how democratic comprehensives have developed. The first is by saying that democratization is part of an *alternative movement*. The second says that there have been particular *historical moments*. The third suggests that there is a *working model* of democratization for schools.

The alternative-movement argument rests upon a recognition that there have been, throughout the twentieth century, revitalized conceptions of education and radical criticisms of its orthodox forms. There is a thread running through educational writings concerned with 'person-centredness', 'dialogue in learning', 'creativity' and 'celebration of awareness'. The works of Montessori, Froebel and Dewey have been linked with those of A.S. Neill and, more recently, Kohl and Freire. These works are part of an aware teacher's sources of inspiration. Each generation of committed teachers connects with this movement and some add to it significantly. Thus Stewart Wilson in 1980 said:

> the school community should come together to build a new democratic society where real social justice, real equality of opportunity and real living are found.

> The main job is to remove all the artificial barriers which have been created over the years in the world of education [for any school which has aspirations to be a real community school]. These barriers are manifold:

> 1. the barrier we have put up around our educational buildings, our schools if you like.
> 2. the barrier we have put up to other sections of the community.
> 3. the barrier which we have erected around ourselves as teachers with regard to our teaching role.
> 4. the barrier with which we have surrounded the curriculum of the school and the subject syllabuses.
> 5. the barrier we have put up around the young people in our schools as though they become different animals once they step inside the school.
> 6. the barriers which often exist between a head and staff and between different departments in the school.

> And what about the biggest barrier of all – our professional training which tells us that we are equipped to teach young people between the ages of eleven and sixteen in a building which shall be called a school. Isn't the community our classroom? . . . Isn't the living community the real starting and finishing point for our science and geography, history and environmental studies teaching? Isn't this the real world which our pupils should be looking at and listening to and thinking about? (Wilson 1980).

The alternative movement is expressed as both commitment and criticism: the commitment to the joy and hope which *can* be realized in learning and the criticism of the cruelty to which it is often put. While Wilson pointed to the barriers in English schools, Mackenzie (1977) wrote of

> Scotland's schools, inflexible, lacking in self-criticism, always with the assumption of righteous indignation, blaming the pupils, unable to adapt themselves to new circumstances of living . . . and be replaced by a totally different way of bringing up children, more flexible, more open-minded, kindlier.

The balance in the alternative movement is between the beauty which is possible and the brutality which is practised in most schools. It is not a movement for opting out of state education but a movement for radically changing it.

Having quoted Mackenzie and Wilson as authorities, it is appropriate to turn to the second kind of explanation, that of the historical moment. This argument says that when the time is right, great people come forward and do great things. There is said to be a synchronism between a major reorganization or the opening of a new school, local officials and politicians enthusiastic for innovation and experimentation, equally as enthusiastic hand-picked staff, and the appointment of a headteacher who inspires confidence in doing things with vigour and vision. Such was said of Stewart Wilson at Sutton Centre. So, too, it was said of Tim McMullen at Countesthorpe College, who wrote (1974): 'We have a chance to rethink the total process of learning within a school . . . it should mean that we do not automatically repeat an established practice without considering why.'

In his Director of Education's view (quoted by Birnbaum 1975): 'Having built a school that is so obviously on the side of the trends in which education appears to be moving . . . we would be looking for somebody who was in sympathy with the changes . . . and we would very much like to have somebody who is a bit ahead.'

The historical moment can be one brief second in generally darker times. Local political control may only fleetingly rest with a group which is against tradition. Legislation changes may carry small sums of money which can be used to great effect. It may excite some to refer to a great experiment taking place. It may equally distress others to hear talk of experiments.

The very moment to which the beginnings of democratization can be traced reveals debate over the suitability of the candidates for headteacher, their philosophies and their political wisdom. In effect, the clearer the head is about a working model for the school, the more the likelihood of polarization during the process of their appointment. Once appointed, though, those with clear working models believe they have sufficient support to put them into practice.

The models themselves are not timeless masterpieces. They might focus upon the key symbolic act of rejecting corporal punishment. In the 1960s, R.F. Mackenzie of Summerhill Academy was exhorting 'teachers of the world unite, you have nothing to lose but your canes'. In the early 1960s, Michael Duane at Risinghill School (quoted in Berg 1968) listed features which included:

- No caning or expulsion
- Pastoral duties for heads of houses
- A School Council of four teachers, three other adults and twelve pupils.
- Flexible opening times
- Open access to parents without appointment.
- Humanist assemblies
- Use of mother tongue in multiracial teaching
- Developing an arts centre and a community centre.

In the late 1960s, McMullen's (1968) principles for Countesthorpe were:

- the whole academic emphasis will be on the individual learning, not the teachers teaching, the intrinsic motivation rising out of the child's curiosity, desire and achievement . . .
- the school and community will be one unit.

To these ends

- there would be four periods a day of 80 minutes each.
- a common core curriculum of four basic subjects and three interdisciplinary subjects.
- all pupils would have periods of independent study time.
- the 'Moot' of all staff to meet weekly and be the main legislative body.

Finally, in the early 1970s, Stewart Wilson (1980) itemized:

- the common system of examining at 16+
- mixed ability teaching
- block timetabling
- the opening of educational premises for 360 days a year
- joint adult and student classes
- and the abolition of corporal punishment.

All four headteachers quoted insisted that their approach to democratization was as a working model. Their models combined directions for the school to develop with achievements for it to recognize. They rejected the historical moment argument as a confusion of their rational advocacy with a personality cult. (Those who are the most personally effective usually reject individualistic explanations the most forcefully.) They also rejected the reduction of their models to the mechanics of aims and objectives. They were aware that expressing aims as targets and objectives as stages towards them is a technique in demonstrating relative failure as well as an adherence to a fixed point of arrival, which takes no account of what has been learned in the meantime. Instead, they spoke of achievements, of what can be learned from the best experiences of teachers and pupils, and how they thought that their directions encouraged more good experiences for more participants. Their working models were not a jumble of boxes whose inhabitants were besieging each other with interaction arrows. Their models tied broad principles to basic provisions – without a lot of modifications in between one and the other.

Trials of democratic comprehensives – and their avoidance

Democratic comprehensives have within their orbit, as teachers, parents and politicians, those who, at first, do not want them to succeed and then actively campaign for their failure. They come from either the crumbling middle class or are first-generation 'white-collar' workers. Small shopkeepers, factory supervisors and office workers seldom want comprehensive education. Nor do they believe that it will produce the discipline, the qualifications and the social-status attainments which they fervently seek for their children. A few such parents combine in a coalition. They have energy and knowledge of the system. They are articulate, impossible to placate, and devoted to their chosen task of opposing the head by finding more and more things wrong with the school. The greater their direct contact with the school, the larger their collection of damning evidence.

Within 'advocacy democratic comprehensives' after a period of increasing anxiety, those who John Watts has called 'a passing coalition of malcontents' find an action which they regard as an outrage. At Risinghill (1961) it was a survey on racialism. At Summerhill (1968) a pupil threatened a teacher with a knife. At Countesthorpe (1973) there were thefts from the library. For Sutton Centre in 1977 the 'trigger event' was a lesson about swearing. Each time the deeper issues were symbolized by the event, but it is the latter which is made the undeniable cause for complaint. Once identified, it never diminished in significance. If it is denied, then there was a cover-up. If it was acknowledged, then there was an admission of guilt.

The mistake became the key evidence in a 'trial by media'. The head, like a standard bearer, is interviewed and appears at emergency meetings. The head is angry about accusations, proud of the school, and worried about the effects of adverse publicity on its working relationships. In the popular press, the controversy is reported like a battle between gladiators in a Roman amphitheatre. In the quality press there is sonorous concern. The media, by either pillorying the head or insisting on balancing the two sides, makes sure the school never wins.

The major form of professional defence, an official inspection, can limit the damage but it cannot repair it all. While the inspection is taking place changes are made. However an inspection happens, the head leaves and so do other teaching staff. The main feature of the trials is that never, not once, were schools tried for advocating democratic comprehensives – not even by their professional peers.

The lessons from such trials are obvious. Have as little as possible to do with a small number of volatile, and socially insecure, adults. Avoid the trigger event and using local media. Have little faith in professional defences – they protect officials not activists.

Advocacy democratic comprehensives roll back the boundaries of innovation for all state secondary schools. Ten or twenty years later some of their processes may be accepted professional practices. In the meantime, they add one more revolution to the alternative movement and have the respect of many teachers for doing so.

How, then, does the experience of advocacy democratic schools relate to the democratization process at large? First, there is the relief of not having to be false, of not needing to hide behind an alien image of teacher or pupil or parent. Just as there is comfortable clothing instead of uniforms there is more energy and encouragement for self-examination and self-criticism. Thinking can and should develop – and out loud! So, too, the right to free expression of opinions is linked to the right to make mistakes, own up to them, and repair the damage yourself.

Beyond self-image, self-esteem and self-expression is the right to associate freely with others, teachers with teachers, pupils with pupils. Friendships are not conspiracies and interest groups can make open alliances. There is debate in place of depression. The debate can lead to changes in practices so that there is participation in the effects. The participants are not locked into their pasts but trying to take their present concerns into concrete provisions for the future. It has always amazed me, for example, that these individual and collective qualities of the social processes of democratization are revered in adult life and feared within schools. Advocacy democratic schools are simply saying that citizens' rights should be found and taken forward in the institutional roles of teacher and pupil. They are made distinctive in schools and are being contributed to at the same time.

In comparison, it is hard not to sound bitter about ambiguously democratic schools. Yet they are less well favoured, usually existing schools rather than new ones, in which the new head was expected to liven things up but not to set them on fire. The staff are a mixture of hard-bitten people who have been there for years and the really caring staff who have the same length of service. There is suspicion about bringing new people in and the dualism of the head's oppor-tunities to make internal promotions. The dualism is that the divided staff has its own nominees and *bêtes noires*. Every promotion is a victory for some and an omen for others. Generally speaking there is less grasp of an alternative movement amongst the staff and some repugnance towards a working model of a democratic comprehensive – at least on the part of a significant few.

The distinction between advocacy and ambiguity goes deeper than staff divisions and adopting a low profile with the local media. It is to be found in the languages used to explain the school's purposes. Advocacy schools reject the idea that their pupils are miniature employees and regard them as micro-citizens. They claim that discipline is part of what is learned, learning *is* self-discipline. So, too, they claim that examination successes are a by-product of wider achievements in confidence, in the capability for reasoned argument, in learning how to learn. In a word, their purpose is empowerment (O'Hagan 1987).

An ambiguous school's staff is more likely to profess the purposes of enrichment and efficiency. By enrichment they mean con-tact with, and encouragement towards, quality in thinking. By efficiency they mean capability in specific marketable tasks and a sensible attitude towards such competences. What makes the school ambiguous is that it will use either or both purposes at different times with the same people. As if in one breath, the listener will be told that the pupils should be more civilized and more qualified, more socially acceptable and more economically viable. The purpose of empower-ment will be kept far in the background. The prospects of enabling pupils from 'disadvantaged homes', of participants 'having a say in running the school' and of local social change through the school becoming a resource in current issues, are all purposes with restricted discussion, if discussed at all.

In this way, ambiguous schools can 'sell' block timetables, team teaching, school councils and the like. They avoid confrontations by claiming that such practices are professionally acknowledged as effective for the purposes of enrichment or efficiency or both. Thus the practices have a dynamic of their own development, rather than profound implications for each other. Ambiguously democratic comprehensives may develop an expertise in the minutiae of such practices. Yet whether they are fitted in like spare-part surgery or fixated upon as crucial to enrichment and efficiency, their origin remains that of empowerment (see, for example, Fletcher 1980).

Put crudely, advocacy schools are politically aware whilst ambiguity schools are professionally centred. The political awareness of advocacy schools may have altered from social change in the 1960s to community education and community development in the 1970s and towards race and gender discriminations in the 1980s. The professional focus of ambiguously democratic schools may have altered from form to content: from school government to curriculum. It is an open question as to whether ambiguous schools can contain their ambiguity until better times, or can live so long in ambiguity without losing sight of empowerment altogether. They should, however, escape being put on trial.

My parents, I think, would have been divided over advocacy – empowerment and ambiguity–enrichment. But their own struggle was with democratically antagonistic schools. In their time there were no advocacy democratic secondary schools. By 1989, in England and Scotland, we have moved from there being none to a period of a few brightly shining examples with some ambiguously democratic secondary schools behind picking up their pieces.

References

Berg, Leila (1968). *Risinghill: Death of a Comprehensive*. London, Penguin.

Birnbaum, G. (1975). 'Countesthorpe College', in A. Harris, M. Lawn and W. Prescott (eds), *Curriculum Innovation*. London, Croom Helm.

Fletcher, Colin (1980). 'The Sutton Centre profile', in T. Burgess and E. Adams (eds), *Outcomes of Education*. London, Macmillan.

Fletcher, Colin, Caron, Maxine and Williams, Wyn (1985). *Schools on Trial: the Trials of Democratic Comprehensives*. Milton Keynes, Open University Press.

Mackenzie, R.F. (1977). *The Unbowed Head: Events at Summerhill Academy 1968–74*. Edinburgh University Student Publications Board.

McMullen, Tim (1968). 'Flexibility for a comprehensive school', *Forum*, 10 (2), 64–7.

McMullen, Tim (1974). 'The education of the uninterested', W.B. Curry Lecture, University of Exeter.

O'Hagan, G.R. (1987). 'Efficiency, enrichment, empowerment', *Journal of Community Education*, 6 (1), 2–5.

Wilson, Stewart (1980). 'The school and the community', in Colin Fletcher and Neil Thompson (eds), *Issues in Community Education*. London, Falmer Press.

Watts, J. (1977). *The Countesthorpe Experience*. London, Allen & Unwin.

CHAPTER 11

Participation and preparation

(i) Helping pupils to help themselves: pupils' councils and participation

Nils Danielsen

Danish law requires all schools to establish a pupils' council. These councils are typically made up of two elected pupils from each of the classes between the sixth grade (12-year-olds) and the tenth grade (16-year-olds). So far, so good! But a remark often to be heard in most schools, all over Denmark, is as follows: 'Our pupils' council doesn't work!' And it is natural to ask, as we have done, why? Why don't pupils' councils work?

Among other things, a frequent explanation is that there is something wrong with the belief that just because pupils have been elected to a council, the following will automatically arise. That these pupils will possess a good and necessary knowledge of the structure of the school and how decisions are made within that structure. That they will have mastered the techniques of running meetings and of working as a council. And that they will feel safe and accepted by each other, despite differences in age and familiarity. In addition, certain practical difficulties arise. Pupils' council might need help in writing out agendas and in keeping minutes; they may be uncertain about how to distribute business arrangements and outcomes of discussion; and they will inevitably lack certain powers for calling pupils' representatives to the committees of the school or the council.

With the intention of facing these difficulties or similar problems, many schools in Denmark have established a contact-teacher system. In general this system is based upon an approach by which certain teachers are specifically charged with developing pupils' influence. Normally the 'contact-teacher' is elected by and from the teachers' council and has to report on his or her work at teacher council meetings. The contact-teacher is charged with the task of supporting the work of the pupils' council by functioning as the administration for the council and its executive committee. They also arrange courses for the council, courses which aim to help members of the council to get to know each other and to better understand the organization of their school and courses which are designed to help representatives to practise political debate and to learn what possibilities are available for their council itself.

To give some idea of how the contact-teacher system operates, in what follows, I will describe just what happened in one year at Stavnsholtskolen, Farum.

One year with the pupils' council

Even before the summer holidays, the new 6th–10th classes have elected two representatives for the pupils' council. The council (about 36 pupils) is invited to a two–day course at the very beginning of the school year. This course takes place in the facilities of the Continuation School in another part of the town, which makes it a real course, away from everyday school.

At the course the pupils are provided with knowledge of the importance of the council in the school system, of its own rules and of pupils' organizations such as LOE and FLO (the pupils' unions). The pupils meet the president of the teachers' council who is on a panel, together with the presidents of the parent–teacher committee and the education committee.

At the course, the pupils council begins to work out a list of tasks its members want to address. This plan-for-the-year means that the pupils' council always has something to do. When urgent matters of current interest have been dealt with, the year–plan is studied. This plan is copied and placed in the representatives' council folder. A very important part of the course is a complete pupils' council meeting which the contact-teacher uses as a basis for exploring meetings and debating techniques.

The two–day course begins with role-play and simulation exercises. These help the pupils to get to know one another and to discover each other's opinions. This means that the last item of the course, which is election for different posts, can take place on a reasonable basis. At this stage the members of the pupils' council are very enthusiastic and most elections are hotly contested.

The daily work of the pupils' council

The executive committee of the pupils' council makes a point of summoning the full council shortly after the course is completed. The agenda for the meeting has one permanent item, 'News from the Committees'. This prevents the appointed committees and the representatives from the committees of the school from neglecting their duties and it reminds them of the importance of informing the pupils' council. Most topics debated by the pupils' council are sent to the classes for discussion before the council comes to a decision at a later meeting.

After agreeing on a proposal, the pupils will pass their ideas on to the appropriate body in the school. Members of the council have to get used to writing letters – a written question demands a written answer and can often expose certain uncertainties more sharply than a spoken message.

The contact-teacher will see to it that the administrative office in the school gives the pupils' council the same support as is given to the teachers' council with respect to such issues as the writing-out of agendas, minutes and the like. Agendas and minutes are distributed by having a call made on the loudspeaker system of the school. A marking system provides a survey of the classes that haven't collected their papers. In addition, minutes of the pupils' council meetings are sent to class teachers of the 6th–10th grades and are displayed on the teachers' noticeboard.

The executive committee of the council has a weekly meeting at which the full council's work is discussed and prepared and where letters to be presented to the council are drafted out. In this way, it is possible for the pupils' council to take an interest in an extensive range of school matters.

The tasks of the pupils' council

The council will discuss any event happening in the school. For instance, it may suggest topics or themes for 'feature-weeks', it may evaluate the annual sports day or it may join in the work of the committee of cultural affairs. Other questions arise:

'Is the information about the subjects you may choose in the 8th–10th classes sufficient?'

'Are we to have one or two terminal examinations in the 9th class?'

'Are there other examples of discussion topics for the pupils' council?'

An adopted resolution of allocating one weekly lesson per class for open discussion caused a lively debate in the classes and the pupils' council. The purpose and importance of school subjects were debated and the observations of the pupils' council gained support from the parent–teacher committee. The renovation of a living-room in which pupils may spend time during the breaks was another task of the pupils' council.

The pupils' council now manage far more tasks than they did previously. One reason for this is the desire of the parent–teacher committee to know the attitude of the pupils' council to as many subjects as possible.

Attending a course again!

The pupils' council hold a monthly meeting. Camps, practical trainee work, holidays and end of term examinations, however, interrupt the work. These interruptions sometimes threaten the stability of the pupils' council work. Partly because of that, we find that a second course for the pupils' council is of great importance. This course-day takes place in February or March, and its purpose is to evaluate the time which has passed since the first course. Members thoroughly discuss the course of pupils' council meetings, the results and the level of co-operation with other parties in the school.

Evaluations have generally been very positive, and, proud of its own results, the pupils' council looks forward to the work of the spring term. Tasks are finished and pupils heading for examinations are replaced by younger persons in the different committees. The election of members for the following year's pupils' council takes place on the 1st of May at the latest, and new members are invited to attend the final meeting of the old council.

The pupils' council's own lesson

The contact-teacher system has improved the workings of the pupils' council. Difficulties arise, however, when topics are to be discussed in the classes during the pupils' own lesson. The working methods of the pupils' council (having a chair and a reporter) has had some influence on the pupils' own lessons, but it is still difficult for the two pupils' council members to make their classmates take an interest in the pupils' council work. The reason for this is partly the nature of representative democracy (of course, it is more fun when you take part yourself) and partly that most of the topics from the pupils' council are so complicated that the representatives have difficulty in explaining them. However, the pupils' council has tried to awaken the interest of other pupils in different ways. The best procedure seems to be the holding of frequent meetings for all the pupils in the 7th–10th classes as a supplement to council work that takes place in the pupils' own lesson.

The contact-teacher's role

The contact-teacher tries to ensure that tasks concerning school administration are dealt with. At the pupils' council meetings the contact-teacher is at the pupils' disposal when they need guidance, although the contact-teacher only contributes if important information is lacking in the debate or if the pupils' council needs guidance about voting or protecting minority interests.

After council meetings, the reporter will need the help of the contact-teacher to make sure that the minutes which are sent out for discussion in the classes are precise and correct. Other tasks for the contact-teacher are to inform other teachers about the work of the pupils' council, to give support to the pupils on boards and in committees, and to ensure that decisions made in the pupils' council are realized.

The contact-teacher's duties as regards the pupils' council can be compared with those of the education committee and headmaster as regards the parent–teacher committee. The popularly elected are those to decide, and it is the official's duty to see that the basis for making decisions is a secure one.

The importance of the contact-teacher system to the school and the pupils

It is very satisfactory that the pupils' council, which represents the numerically largest group in school, should express opinions about school matters. For nearly all the pupils who take part in the work of the pupils' council it is true to say that the work gives them their first experiences of spheres of interest and organization. These experiences can be decisive in motivating them to join organizing work at

some other time and place, be it party-political, grass-roots movements, or trade union work.

The contact-teacher system for the pupils' council has meant that
some pupils devote quite a lot of their energies and their ideas to the
pupils' council and, through that, the school. And it seems re-
freshing and renewing when pupils reflect on how to make *their*
school better.

(ii) The need for a pupils' statute in a democratic school

Frederik Smit

Danielsen's account of how the contact-teacher system at Stavnsholt
School helps to support the smooth functioning of the pupils'
council (see above) provides us with some clear ideas of how these
councils can be made more effective. Danielsen suggests that one
obstacle to the effective operation of pupils' councils is that, often,
the pupils themselves lack the skills necessary to run councils and to
organize proper discussion. Furthermore, pupils often have only a
limited understanding of the ins and outs of how their school works
and are thus limited in the contribution they can make to the
decision-making process. It seems obvious, therefore, that pupils'
councils need guidance from teachers. At Stavnsholt the basic aim
was to use teachers as a resource to give pupils the necessary
knowledge, skills and support required for their council to become
an effective and functioning democratic influence. This approach
was obviously very valuable. However, I wish to argue that, on its
own, it is not enough if one wishes to strengthen the pupils' weak
position in the organization of a school and to involve these pupils as
equal partners, with adults, in the crucial area of decision-making.
What pupils also need is clarification of their legal status at school.

Pupils' rights and duties

It appears that when pupils take a seat on a pupils' council they find it
important to know where they stand with regards to their exact

rights and duties as pupils at school. Pupils' representatives in pupils' councils feel a need to know exactly what possibilities they have to act as representatives of the pupils, how they can best stand up for pupils' rights and what authority they have. In most schools these matters lack clarity.

A well-defined legal status of pupils is in accordance with a democratically functioning school. It also fits in nicely with the view that pupils as young citizens demand a recognizable place of their own in the social context within which they function. Of course, discussions about the legal status of pupils in the educational system are as old as the system itself. What educational system would there be without any pupils?

Until, let us say, the end of the sixties, pupils were mainly considered as more or less passive consumers. They were offered X number of available courses, which they were allowed to make use of, and that was about it. From the end of the sixties – especially under the influence of the general 'wave of democratization' – this view began to change somewhat. There was an increasing awareness that pupils not only have duties but also rights, and that as part of the school community they should be involved in matters that concern them. At many schools in The Netherlands these issues came into the open – sometimes through school or students' papers, sometimes through school 'parliaments' or pupils' councils. During this period one sometimes came across the term 'pupils' statute'. Such a statute is the whole collection of rules and regulations which define a pupil's legal status at school; they embody both pupils' rights and pupils' duties and thus the rights and duties of other members of the school community, in relation to the pupils. The Education Participation Act of 1981 actually made the first real formal acknowledgement of the fact that pupils ought to be involved in major school issues. It was also in this Act that the term 'pupils' statute' was first mentioned. It is only from 1984 onwards that the necessity of a pupils' statute began to evolve. It seems inevitable that after prisoners, patients, consumers and soldiers, it is now the turn of the legal status of pupils to receive the attention to which it is entitled.

The importance of a pupils' statute

In the educational process in which teachers and pupils are involved, different roles, rules and regulations are inevitable. Education is primarily an interaction between human beings, human beings involved in the process of transfer and development of knowledge and insight, and of behaviour and values. The educational process takes place within the framework of an educational organization. Rules can create unambiguous relations at school. Rules by themselves cannot change power relations at school, but what they can do is make them identifiable. Drawing up rules and regulations is synonymous with a moment of reflection on relations inside a school. Rules in school concern the school as a social community and they also have to do with the school as a learning community. In general, social rules and regulations will be similar to those of other big organizations. But, the rules and regulations for learning relate quite specifically to the educational process itself.

It is important to have a pupils' statute at school because, like teachers and parents, pupils are equally entitled to a proper and well-defined legal status. Within the school environment, pupils are also entitled to a recognizable and protected position of their own. In a pupils' statute, the rights and duties of pupils can be clarified and improved. For pupils this implies that:

- a pupils' statute can give shape to the educational climate at school in which the pupil is taken seriously. A pupils' statute can provide room for the development of each pupil,
- in a pupils' statute equality can be expressed between all the parties involved in the learning process. Constitutional rights, such as freedom of speech, are rights for all citizens, regardless of age. Constitutional rights must also be respected at school,
- a pupils' statute fits within a democratic structure at school. Pupils are citizens who are in the process of growing up; a democratic school prepares for and is part of a democratic society. Democracy is not only a form of administrative organization in which all participants have a say, but it is also a community, in which rights and duties between the authorities (in whatever form) and citizens are described precisely and with criteria that can be easily judged,
- a pupils' statute is concerned with the rights and duties of the pupil towards the school staff/management and the teachers at a school, and vice versa.

Items for a pupils' statute

The schedule below mentions the areas which might be the proper concern of a pupils' statute. For the pupils they will lead to more clarity, insight and legal security in the educational system. Items for a pupils' statute:

Admission: the criteria of admission, the procedures of admission and the possibilities of appeal in case of non-admission.

Information: regulations in relation to the oral and written supply of information and consultation hours for pupils.

Expression of opinions: the editorial status of the school paper and any pupils' magazine and the use of notice-boards.

Freedom of assembly: the use of (class) rooms at school, the use of equipment, the founding of a pupils' council.

Protection of privacy: the responsibility of the management for and the admission to record systems, possibilities of verification by those involved (pupils and parents), the right to delete false and outdated information.

Discipline inside the schools: the legal liability of school management and teachers, the contents of disciplinary rules and the nature of sanctions (impositions, staying behind), those empowered to impose sanctions (staff, including teachers and other members of staff), the procedures of sanction (possibilities of reviewing or suspending decisions) and possibilities of appeal.

Presence at school: being late, attendance at class, staying at school in case of cancelled and free periods, informing parents of absence without leave, days off and occasional holidays.

Behaviour and appearance: freedom of appearance, dress regulations in relation to hygiene or safety regulations (PE practical lessons), opportunities for body-care (toilet usage), use of alcohol, tobacco, drugs and so on, eating, drinking and having sweets in class and in and around school.

Outdoor activities: possibilities for organizing outdoor activities, responsibilities for outdoor activities, the financial obligations.

Proper education: the binding effects of the school curriculum, formulating the criteria for 'proper education', possibilities for pupils to question the quality of education.

Assessment of education: timely announcement of test results, the contents of test papers and their relation to the lessons taught, the ways of and criteria for assessment, the possibility of re-doing test papers, procedures in case of absence (e.g. because of illness), the procedure in cases of cheating, the obligation of teachers to give results of a test paper within a certain time period, the possibility of lodging an appeal against the ways of assessment and grading, the possibilities of lodging an appeal with an arbitration board.

School reports: the relevance of reports and of report marks, the ways of calculating report marks, discussion of reports.

Selection of schools, subjects and types of school: the criteria for the selection of types of school and subjects, ways in which a pupil can voice a preference, the way in which parents can voice their preferences, the procedure and final decision.

Homework: the obligation to do homework, the 'homework period' on the timetable, the overall load of homework, spreading homework tasks, the possibility of being exempted from homework as a special way of giving leave.

School-ombudsman: a confidential and independent person, either from within or from outside the school community who can be consulted in cases of communication problems or conflicts.

Arbitration board: the setting up of an arbitration board which assesses whether certain behaviour by a pupil, a teacher, a staff member, or a member of the school management, or someone else from the school community is subjected. An arbitration board should be independent and should, at the same time, be representative of the school community.

Suspension and expulsion: the kinds of behaviour which may lead to the sanctions of suspension and expulsion, the criteria which may lead to expulsion for low achievement at school, the procedures and possibilities of appeal, announcements of suspensions and expulsions.

A pupils' statute will have to be the result of a process of discussion and of decision-making at every school. Specification and formulation will be closely related to the atmosphere and the size of the school in question. Maybe, it is very sensible to give the pupils' statute a limited period of validity, for example, two years. The experience thus gained can be incorporated after that period of time. Every year there will be a shift of pupil members; also fresh pupils should be constantly involved in their own statute.

On the basis of the findings of the contact-teacher system with pupils' committees in Denmark and the experience with pupils' councils at Dutch schools, the following recommendations can be postulated:

1. At each school a pupils' statute will have to be drawn up in which the pupils' rights and duties in all the various fields are recorded.
2. Pupil members of a pupils' council should be given the opportunity to attend training courses because there is a demonstrable need for them to obtain knowledge and skills, in order to be able to participate in decision-making processes at school.
3. The role of the pupils' council must be well defined so that a clear division of tasks can be brought about between the pupils'

council, the parent–teacher committee, the teachers' council and staff/management.

4. In order to prepare for meetings of the pupils' council, pupils should receive necessary information from staff and school management in good time and without them having to ask for it so that they can consult fellow pupils, obtain additional information and can consult 'experts', if necessary.

5. The agenda of the pupils' councils should not only be distributed among members, but also among fellow pupils. This guarantees that everyone will be informed about the time, place and items on the agenda of the meetings in question.

6. Every school year, the pupils' council should write an annual report on its activities and results so that these become real and noticeable to pupils, parents and staff members at school.

Conclusion

For pupils, school is not only a place for the transfer of knowledge, skills and perceptions, but it is also used by them as a place to meet people of the same age, a place that is suitable for them to experiment and to come face to face with different ways of life. Education should provide for space for a youth culture of its own, space that should be given at school. A pupils' statute may express ways in which this space is formally defined. It can contribute to a smooth way of running things at school and can give support to pupils in their experience of how a democratic school can function.

(iii) Helping teachers to help themselves: democracy and teacher-training

Stephen Walker and Hans Jorgen Kristensen

Democratic education and teacher attitudes – Stephen Walker

Every year, as someone not only concerned with the development of democratic schooling and open learning but also involved in teacher-training, I am faced with something of a dilemma, something of a puzzle. The problem arises from trying to understand the responses made by new entrants to the teaching profession, student-teachers, to ideas about democratic education. Every year, as an essential first step in an induction programme for new students, I ask these prospective teachers to indicate and defend the kind of teacher they will strive to become, in terms of a model of teacher types. The model, developed by M. Hammersley (1977) contains shorthand descriptions of identifiable teacher 'types' and brings together ideas and approaches in teaching which group around four distinctive visions of an ideal teacher. The four types, which are represented on a continuum which begins with the authoritarian teacher who uses hierarchically structured methods and materials and moves through to the democratic teacher who uses collaborative methods, are called:

- discipline-based teaching
- programmed teaching
- progressive teaching, and
- radical non-interventionist.

Every year, without fail, almost all the students reject the radical non-interventionist and strongly identify themselves with the 'progressive' stance in the model. So what is the dilemma here? The problem is that these students will *agree* with the logic of the ideas associated with the radical non-interventionist but see no prospect of implementing such ideas and, worse, that during their training, many students seem to move away from the progressive ideal towards the programmed-teaching type as a description of the kind of teacher they are likely to become. The question, therefore, is what persuades these new teachers to embrace this perspective of teaching and why do they appear to reject ideas about their work which challenge the status quo in schools rather than confirm it?

To some extent, these student attitudes might simply be reflections of their own experience as pupils of the 'undemocratic' ethos of English classrooms and school. To read *official* statements about English schooling, one would be forgiven for imagining that these describe a system deliberately designed to be broadly in sympathy with the aim of promoting independence and initiative and the opposition to authoritarian, didactic methods which are characteristic of democratic educational goals. Thus, for example, in DES *The Curriculum from 5 to 16* (1985), an official discussion paper paving the way for the current crusade in English educational politics – the development and implementation of a centrally controlled and standardized national curriculum – it is boldly asserted that:

> Schools, homes and society at large are at pains to encourage values and qualities in pupils which will result in attitudes characteristic of a good citizen in a democratic, humane and free society. Some examples of such qualities are reliability, initiative, self-discipline and tolerance. They may be encouraged in the formal curriculum and the informal, and in the general life of the school.

and that a major system goal is 'to help pupils develop lively, enquiring minds, the ability to question and argue rationally and to apply themselves to tasks'. Despite this kind of rhetoric, however, both research evidence (Sharp and Green 1975; Ball 1981; Burgess 1983) and personal experience testify to a reality in the vast majority of English schools which is typified by alienation, hierarchical organization, unequal interpersonal relations between teachers and pupils and between pupils and pupils, authoritarian rule systems, rituals and routines, and a strong 'academic' orientation in the curriculum.

Of course, this is not to say that there have not been important and influential democratic *movements* in English schooling, some which continue and others which have been contained or crushed. For the purpose of this discussion, it is useful to distinguish three separate kinds of action upon which attempts at democratization have been attempted – the first at the level of the education system, the second at the level of the school, and the third related to specific issues and individual attitudinal reform. It is worth considering these broad movements for a moment because by identifying those elements in them which survived and won popular and professional support, by uncovering what gets tolerated, it might be possible to detect those influences which work upon the student-teachers with whom I am concerned.

At the level of the education system, two related post-war reforms which involved a push towards the democratization of education were the move to establish *'progressive' methods* in primary schools (5–11 age-range) and the reorganization of secondary schooling (11–16) on comprehensive lines. Progressive primary education won official support in the celebrated Plowden Report (1967), which affirmed that:

> The school sets out deliberately to devise the right environment for children, to allow them to be themselves and to develop in the

way and at the pace appropriate to them. It tries to equalize opportunity and to compensate for handicaps . . . A child brought up in such an environment . . . has some hope of becoming a balanced and mature adult and of being able to look critically at the society of which he [*sic*] forms a part.

Child-centred learning, self-discovery, initiative, individual learning patterns, curriculum choice, integrated learning schemes, informal teaching, integrated topics were watchwords in the concern to meet the idiosyncratic requirements of childhood. Formality, rigidity and adult imposition were rejected. Meanwhile, in secondary education, comprehensive reorganization was being established – and drawing on visions of the elimination of class inequalities, the integration of local communities and the removal of barriers to personal self-development – non-selective, community comprehensive schools were created throughout the system. Ball (1981) suggests that three models of comprehensive principles emerged:

- the Meritocratic, concerned with equality of opportunity,
- the Integrative, concerned with improving tolerance,
- the Egalitarian, concerned with promoting educational change and democracy in schools as the main *means* to increased equality and integration outside education.

It is, perhaps, significant that the last of these, the Egalitarian proved to be the basis for very few real schools.

It has to be said that both these movements in English education have lost their influence and impetus. In primary schools, normal practice currently involves a skill-based, hierarchical curriculum which emphasizes literacy and numeracy, fixed-ability grouping in classroom, a low degree of pupil participation in decision-making and some preference for didactic teaching. In many, many comprehensive schools, one finds a return to streaming, to an examination- and subject-dominated curriculum and to closed relations with local communities.

One reason for this 'failure' must be that progressivism and comprehensive thinking posed too great a threat to the state's interest in the school system. In this respect, it is salutary to observe that current reforms of the education system in the UK being pressed by the Thatcher administration – support to the private sector and to 'creeping privatization', the new vocationalism, the new, single, 16-plus GCSE examination and the new national curriculum – as well as effectively wiping out many of the changes in educational practice accomplished through progressive and comprehensive reform also represent a significant tightening of the ratchet of the state control of education.

A similar fate has befallen a large number of innovatory projects which, seeking to apply certain Egalitarian principles of education in the sense Ball uses the term (above), attempted democratic reform at the level of the school. I have in mind here projects like William Tyndale Primary School, Risinghill, Madeley Court School, Summerhill Academy, Sutton Centre, Countersthorpe College and Stantonbury Campus. Each of these schools (or, more precisely, the particular headteachers of the schools) made different interpretations of democratic schooling and used significantly different starting-points.

William Tyndale School made co-operative teaching and pupil curriculum choice an early target; Risinghill emphasized pupil consultation, participation and equality of treatment; Summerhill Academy had an early focus on curriculum reforms alongside attempts to develop teacher–pupil relations in the school based on mutual respect and trust; Sutton Centre was established as a place which put community needs first and made social education the emphasis in teacher democracy, non-ritualistic teacher–pupil relations and a gradual move to an interdisciplinary curriculum; and innovation at Stantonbury Campus was initiated through curriculum reform in which, through resource-based approaches, the distinction between formal and informal learning was deliberately blurred.

Of all these projects, the first four have been successfully suppressed in various ways and only the Stantonbury programme retains anything like its original design. This is, I think, significant. Of all the projects listed above, this last one was the only one which, ironically for reform aimed at democratization, did not make teacher–pupil relations or pupil 'power' an essential element of the initiative or a key starting-point for change.

One positive outcome of the spread of comprehensive schooling was that it heightened awareness of the problems confronting women and ethnic minorities inside and outside schools. As a result, there has been a steady development of a third approach to democratization, the struggle against gender and race inequalities. In comparison with the first two movements mentioned above, the third level has been comparatively successful. Issues to do with gender, race and education are highly placed on the political and debating agenda in education; they are and have been the subject of considerable legislation since the mid-1970s aimed at providing a basis for action on inequality; they are the subject of both national and local policy initiatives and of the mushrooming equal opportunity appointments and projects in schools and, in period of economic constraint, equal opportunity projects have received special and positive funding in the UK. Given the relative failure of the first two levels of reform I have outlined, one might wonder about the success of this third strand.

To explain this contradiction, it is useful to consider exactly what reforms are being accomplished and the kind of attitudes they provoke in interested parties. Policy debates to do with both race and schooling and gender and schooling are presently sharply divided. In the debate about race relations, the division is between the advocates of multicultural education and of anti-racist education. Multicultural education concentrates on such targets as extending the curriculum to celebrate cultural diversity, developing teaching strategies aimed at building a positive self-image in pupils from ethnic minorities, eradicating bias from teaching materials, supporting bilingual teaching programmes and establishing closer links between schools and minority cultural groups. In direct contrast, anti-racist education attempts to bring the struggle of black people into the school and challenge individual and institutional racism, a white problem, through educational programmes. Such programmes would include challenging racist incidents, developing curriculum material on the nature of white racism and of personal prejudice, making power and opportunity a subject of study in school and encouraging alliances between schools and anti-racist campaigns.

Although there is some evidence that both sides of this debate are being acted upon, perhaps not surprisingly, it is also clear that central government is giving strong financial and political support to multicultural education (by making, for example, £1 million available in 1987 for projects which fit this approach) whilst opposing anti-racist education (even to the petty level of refusing financial support to in-service courses which use these words as a title). There is also evidence that many teacher attitudes match those of the government. In a recent ethnographic study of 'multicultural' practice in schools, Crozier (1988) observes an overwhelming dismissal by teachers of attempts to start anti-racist programmes. This attitude seemed to be based upon resentment at apparently being blamed for wider 'social ills', a lack of awareness of racism and, importantly, their deep allegiance with the multicultural stance. There is, Crozier suggests, 'a common code or ideology of multicultural education which has been taken on board by teachers uncritically but in the belief that it is both pedagogically and ethically sound'. This code, she believes, is based on the shared aims of

- promoting tolerance,
- improving black pride and self-image,
- ending racism by attacking the ignorance on which it is based, and,
- by promoting respect of 'their' culture

and is evidenced in such teacher statements as

> It's to try to help kids to have an understanding of other beliefs, hoping that it will make them more tolerant, to relate better to each other; to build better understanding between groups. We are trying to relate to them [black children] and for their benefit. The Muslims and Sikhs have got a lot out of it. It gives them identity within their peer group.

Crozier goes on to suggest that her observations of 'multicultural' lessons – distinguished particularly by an emphasis on the exoticism of the minority culture being 'studied', by an emphasis on the cultures being different from 'our way of living', by a sense of 'specialness' of the lessons and by a total neglect of the political context of the cultural phenomenon being explored – support a view that such practice is likely to have a consequence quite opposite to the one intended.

The conservatism evidenced in these teacher attitudes to issues about 'race' relations and schooling is paralleled in the stance adopted by many teachers in the gender debate. Here again, the ranks are divided. Weiner (1986) depicts differences in analysis and in strategy amongst those trying to combat sex differentiation and subordination in schools as a split between the 'Egalitarians' and the 'Radicals'; she claims that, 'Whereas the former have not seriously addressed the relationship between patriarchy, power and women's subordination, the latter have placed it at the centre of their thinking.' Egalitarians adopt an equal-opportunities approach, and press for changes like more girls in science, a move to non-sexist texts, courses and rituals in schools and more equal opportunity in appointments and organization. Radicals adopt an anti-sexist approach, and strive for girl-centred education, a curriculum which includes female experience and the nature of women's oppression, a school organization based on girl-friendly procedures and for programmes in schools which support anti-sexist groups.

In a wider study of teacher attitudes made of my own students last year (Ingleby 1987), we found an almost total affiliation with Egalitarian thinking and a rejection of anti-sexist approaches. All students revealed fairly sharp insights into the links between schooling and sexism, fairly deep feelings of anger at discriminatory practices in school, and clear commitment to the idea of change. However, central to their ideologies of teaching was a notion of moderatism, a fear of taking sides. They cherished a kind of liberalism which was based on a strong desire to avoid indoctrination of their pupils and an assumption that, as professionals, they could be neutral. Feminism was something they did not associate with. Rather, their perspective tended to be that which perceived feminist teachers to be fighting a battle of their own. Typical of their comments are:

> I think everything in moderation. I do like to actively combat racism and sexism, but I'm very aware of giving kids both sides of the coin and not indoctrinating them. The two teachers we had in school were so extreme that they put their opinions across in a negative light in the kids' eyes.

> As long as it's not carried to the extreme and they aren't sexist against men: what they need is to strike a balance.

> I think they are going to bore the poor kids to death. If they make it obvious that they don't want sex inequality they are going to restrict their teaching methods. It should be natural, not too obvious.

The ideas of moderation and subtlety were important to them and influenced how they thought they would provide equality of opportunity – thus:

> I think I treat boys and girls, coloured and anybody . . . I think I treat them all the same. I don't have to think about it, it comes naturally.

> I'd work in little subtle ways . . . not making it too obvious. I think it's all common-sense as far as I'm concerned. If I was unhappy and I could see that there was a case and a need for it, then – of course – I would do something.

> I think it's my common-sense really. I try to do things in my own sort of quiet way rather than going in there and saying 'this is what we are going to do today'. I do things gradually and through different sorts of examples.

And so – to return to the initial dilemma. Does consideration of the conservatism displayed in attitudes to anti-racist and anti-sexist initiatives in education shed any light on the source of the more general caution and conservatism in student-teacher attitudes with which I began this discussion?

To some extent, it is quite possible that *both* forms of conservatism are outcomes of processes which work on teachers during the formation of their professional perspective and culture. One such process is the recruitment patterns typical in teaching. Lortie (1975), for example, has argued that the conservatism, individualism and presentism which he thinks characterize teacher attitudes are reflections of consistently similar influences during recruitment, training and career. According to Lortie, teaching recruits two broad kinds of entrants – those who identify with the school system and those who are indifferent to it. The former are attracted by a service ideal and by the opportunity the job gives for them to continue interests they established as a pupil, by the opportunity to achieve material security and by the opportunity to maintain non-professional interests alongside teaching. The latter are brought to teaching by getting carried along by the academic conveyer-belt whilst failing to secure any alternative to teaching as a pathway to higher education or adult career. Either way, teaching attracts either those keen to conserve existing arrangements in school or those who lack motivation to challenge these traditions.

Conservatism is further reinforced during training – even in institutions which proclaim democratic or progressive educational ideals. Bartholomew (1976) argues that, whatever messages about teaching are proclaimed in the official curriculum of training programmes, the hidden curriculum of teacher-training perpetuates and mystifies conservative educational practice. This hidden curriculum is a consequence of those practices in teacher-training which contradict the ideology of teaching being encouraged at the discursive level, and such practices would include:

- the separation of theory from practice,
- the separation of thought from action,
- the essentially hierarchical structure of the social relations of the educational encounter routine in teacher-training.

I don't want to deny these influences. But, the student-teachers I am anxious to understand are – at a discursive level, at least – scornful of the undemocratic traditions they see in schools, deeply self-critical of their own inability to open up learning experiences and painfully penetrating in their perceptions of the hidden curriculum of their own training. The difficulties they have in accepting and enacting democratic principles are, I think, more fundamental and are partially articulated in the ways in which the teacher and students quoted earlier reveal their dismissal of anti-racist/anti-sexist initiative. Crozier, in her analysis of the 'common code' of multicultural education suggests that it is accepted by teachers because, predicated as it is on a deficit model of pupils (black pupils lack positive self-image, white pupils lack tolerance) it does not challenge common-sense assumptions about the essential purposes and practices of teaching. One of these assumptions, I would suggest, is about the nature, the definition, the view of the pupil or the learner – as being somehow in a *necessarily asymmetrical* relationship with the teacher. The pupil *has* to be defined in some kind of state of need – not necessarily deficient but always in a position of dependency. Otherwise, how can the teacher justify her presence, her effort, her motivation? How can she know her goals? How can she establish a meaningful work identity? Fairly central to the personal teaching ideologies of those student-teachers I have described as rejecting anti-sexist education, is some kind of idea of teaching as a mission. For instance, in talking about the reward of teaching, all students made some kind of reference to their ability and opportunity to *transform* pupils in some way or another. For example:

> Well I need the money but I do find it rewarding as well, when I see the kids getting something out of it . . . I see that I'm educating the kids.

> It's great when the kids know what I'm talking about, or you get a positive response from them to feel that what you are teaching them is sinking in . . . you need it to feel good.

For these student-teachers to admit that the children they were responsible for were not *benefiting* from their contact with them, would have been a denial of their teacher role. Such an assumption makes ideas about pupil-power or pupil-choice or pupil-as-decision-maker incredible and threatening. Of course, we know that when new teachers do gain direct experience of democratically organized schools and collaborative learning in classroom they are able to reinspect such common-sense knowledge. The problem is producing the teachers to produce the situations to produce the experiences to produce the teachers. Catch 22.

Teaching teachers democratically – Hans Jorgen Kristensen

The previous section in this chapter ends with a somewhat gloomy view of the possibilities of training new teachers who are willing to work towards increased democracy in schools. 'The problem', it is suggested, 'is producing the teachers to produce the situations to produce the experiences to produce the teachers.' That the problem exists is undeniable – but it need not be seen as intractable, as insurmountable.

In order to explore some possible ways of lessening the gloom and of cutting into the problem, I would like, first, to phrase the paradox in a slightly different way, to pose a slightly different question. It is this: How might we envisage the kind of qualification we give to new teachers which would prepare them to produce the situations to produce the experiences to produce the teachers?

If a teacher is going to be able to participate in changing schools, in developing democratic principles in education, it seems to me that he or she will have to have at least the following four qualifications:

1. A *personal ideal* of democratic schooling and a personal *commitment* to fight for the ideal. Democracy is not just an ideal or a right; it is a framework for fighting and co-operating in a process which increases the extent and the effectiveness of democratic practice.
2. *Personal experience* of living in an institutional or social structure and of *trying to change these structures* in directions which accord with individual and group goals, and this includes experience of being involved in the decision-making process.
3. The necessary *concepts, tools and skills* to be able to understand different interpretations of democracy and their consequences and to be able to analyse and act within the social structure. These include knowledge of ideas, of power, of laws, and of how institutions operate and strategies and of tactics which can be adapted in an integrated approach drawing upon sources such as political science, philosophy, psychology and sociology.
4. Access to the necessary *conditions* (including access to the power structure) to be able to use the concepts, tools and skills in their struggle towards changing structures in schools and society along democratic lines. In school this means, in essence, that you have to belong to either a majority or minority group which has the strength to seek power and status and the courage to fight for common ideas on democracy and education with patience and with an eye to long-term possibilities.

Clearly, qualifications 1–3 above can be objects of the learning process in teacher-training; qualification 4, however, refers to conditions student-teachers will work with *after* their initial training. Qualification 4, though, is important. Even supposing teachers achieve the first three targets, they can hardly be expected to work in schools in which the majority of colleagues are against change or are anti-democratization without being made progressively less radical (or more 'realistic'!). It is equally clear that, to some extent, the success one has in providing these qualifications depends on the kind of teacher training you have. If you have a training period of, say, four years during which student-teachers are studying both school subjects and teaching methods or pedagogy in a unified course, I would argue that qualifications 1–3 are quite possible achievements (depending on recruitment of initial candidates). If you have a teacher-training period of, say, one year where student teachers study pedagogy separate from their undergraduate courses in academic or school subjects, then the possibilities become more modest.

However, what practical steps can be taken to realize these qualifications? Ideals and attitudes, qualification 1, can be developed in meetings and discussions with tutors and colleagues during training, especially if the learning conditions themselves reflect the direction of the political purposes for which we are striving. To realize the second goal of giving students experience of trying to change everyday life in educational establishments, you must develop within the teacher-training colleges frameworks which are neither too soft or flexible or too hard to change. If the former applies, then student-teachers will not get any experience of fighting against an existing structure. If the latter applies, then the routines, the rules and the attitudes of the staff in the college become the first target. To realize the third goal, of equipping students with a knowledge of practice and of possibilities, it is necessary to establish a curriculum which is interdisciplinary, and where form and content, theory and practice combine.

The last qualification, goal 4, is not strictly a matter for teacher-training as such. Nevertheless, I think the problems and possibilities of political struggle and innovation in schools *are* essential topics for study and for theorizing in teacher-training. Student-teachers must be confronted with the kind of problems they will meet in practice. Only then can they reflect on questions like:

- What kind of teacher do I want to be?
- What kinds of problems and resistances can I cope with without

becoming a kind of teacher I don't want to be?
- Where can I find the groups of friends and professionals I can work with in the struggle to fulfil my own purposes – such as extending democracy in education and education for democracy?

Maybe we need not be quite so gloomy, quite so pessimistic!

References

Ball, S. (1981). *Beachside Comprehensive*. Cambridge, Cambridge University Press.

Bartholomew, J. (1976). 'The myth of the liberal college', in M. Young and G. Whitty (eds), *The Politics of Educational Knowledge*. Driffield, Nafferton.

Burgess, R. (1983). *Experiencing Comprehensive Education*. London, Methuen.

Crozier, G. (1988). 'Multicultural education: some unintended consequences', in S. Walker and L. Barton (eds), *Politics and the Processes of Schooling*. Milton Keynes, Open University Press.

DES (1985). *The Curriculum from 5 to 16: Curriculum Matters 2*. London, HMSO.

Hammersley, M. (1977). *Teacher Perspectives*. Course E202, Unit 9. Open University, Milton Keynes.

HMSO (1967). *Children and their Primary Schools*. The Plowden Report. London, HMSO.

Ingleby, A. (1987). 'The teacher trap: sexism and teacher training'. Unpublished BEd thesis: University of Birmingham (Newman College).

Lortie, D. (1975). *School Teacher*, Chicago. University of Chicago Press.

Sharp, R. and Green, A. (1975). *Education and Social Control*. London, Routledge & Kegan Paul.

Weiner, G. (1986). 'Feminist education and equal opportunities', *British Journal of Sociology of Education*, vol. 7 (3).

CHAPTER 12

Democratization policy and educational theory

Equality and participation: the twofold goal of democratization

Sibe Soutendijk

The two social functions of schooling, reproduction and emancipation, do not appear to be completely opposite to each other. They represent partly different dimensions and refer to two different faces of society: reproduction of inequality refers to the static conception of the stratified society and emancipation to the dynamic conception of a society ruled by power relations. But both social functions have to do with democracy.

1. The social functions turned into positive aims

The social functions of schooling are abstract sociological constructs, defined by their quasi-mechanical effects in society. In order to make them useful for that kind of human action which is aimed at the democratization of education, the social functions have to be redefined as positive aims for democratization.

While reproduction of inequality is defined by negative social effects we have to reverse its tenor. The democratic aim becomes: furthering *equality* by taking educational measures and actions to prevent the reproduction process. This equality aim concerns mainly external democratization, the old 'equal chances' goal. Research outcomes and theoretical analyses in the realm of reproduction

theory offer many suggestions about the specific educational prop-
erties which should be fought, changed, or furthered in order to
reach better educational attainments and, thereby, better social
opportunities for socially disadvantaged children.

The emancipation function is already positive in its social effects.
To turn this function into an aim, we have only to specify the object.
In the beginning, the emancipation function was connected with the
collective emancipation effects of the introduction of compulsory
basic education and the general spread of literacy. Even the gradual
shift in Western societies whereby, in basic education, the reproduction function has become an important *raison d'être* of schooling,
has a kind of positive effect. It has meant that the 'pure' *emancipation*
function is a less official or less noticeable operation, being mainly
related to the supposed effects of any *internal* democratization in a
school and the possible ways in which schools prepare pupils for
collective and individual participation in the adult society. Within
actual education, therefore, we may call the positive emancipation
aim: participation.

The *participation* aim of democratization concerns the fight against
domination. On the one hand, this is a fight for the enhancement of
equal rights and solidarity and for the growth of mutual respect,
shared influence and control amongst pupils, teachers, parents and
members of the local community; a fight within the 'now', the
present conditions of the school society (internal democratization).
On the other hand, it is to do with qualifying pupils so that they can
resist oppression and discrimination and can fight for democratic
participation and influence in their 'later' adult social life.

2. The framework of democratization

Having defined the social objectives of democratization as equality
and participation, we can cross them with the schooling functions of
education: qualification and socialization.

This gives us a basic framework of 'democratization of education
aimed at equality and participation', which is set out in Figure 12.1.
The framework consists of four fields of possibilities open to democratizing innovations. Each field has three overlapping ovals, pro-
visionally filled with some orientating concepts which might be
particular objectives to pursue with the pupils. You have to look at
the scheme with a flexible view. You could include more or less ovals
per field; the number of three is more aesthetic than systematic. You
could insert other more suitable concepts. Our main purpose is to

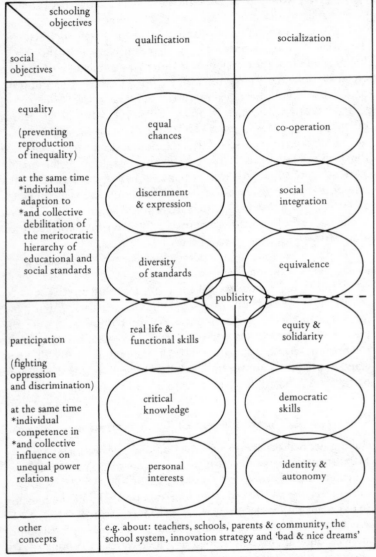

Figure 12.1 Democratization and the functions of schooling – an analytic framework

widen the perspective and to create a broad scale of possibilities. At the same time, it should be kept in mind that the four fields are interdependent. Working in one field, or at one particular objective in a certain way, will bear consequences for other fields or objectives and the boundary between equality and participation is especially fragile and therefore painted by a broken line.

In the next four sections I will explain what I think each aim or oval involves. The overall principle is that we try to specify these aims in such a way that they support or at least don't harm each other.

3. The framework explained: equality qualification

The specification of objectives in the upper half of the scheme, the equality half, can be backed up by the actual outcomes of Dutch investigations, as well as foreign research (Soutendijk 1986). That is because empirical research into democratization of education is mainly done in the ways which relate to the 'equal chances' goal.

Equal chances

Qualification aimed at equality takes the equal–chances goal seriously. Equal chances, however, is in itself an equivocal goal, because the meritocratic standards for educational and social success consist of a mixture of real material or structural inequalities and of social prejudices about the status of professions and other human activities, degrading subordinate groups in the population (cf. Kreckel 1976).

In our case we define equal chances in the traditional way, taking the meritocratic ladder for granted. However, this should be done only on the condition that working at objectives concerning equal chances for the future doesn't lead to a consolidation or even increase of the endemic inequality which is part of meritocratic rule.

Hence, the equal-chances aim within education can be defined as the striving for a more even distribution of girls and boys and of pupils from different social classes and ethnic groups across whatever meritocratic levels are supported by their ultimate educational attainments. But this is not enough. Our endeavour can only prevent enlargement of meritocratic inequality when it is combined with positive action, marked by making an increase in educational attainment of the bottom groups a consistent priority. So, for instance, whilst it is very important to make more immigrant children reach university level and succeed there, it is still more urgent to see to it that none of these children leaves school prematurely, without any qualification (cf. Soutendijk 1986a).

This priority condition makes rather precise demands on the ways schools try to further equal chances. For instance, in so far as achievement differentiation is needed, the principal aim should be to provide extra attention and social support for the children who have the least likelihood of reaching minimal requirements. The school team supports itself in the pursuance of this priority, when it formulates communal objectives for achievements in the basics attached to each year's courses, objectives which are meant to be reached by every pupil.

Discernment and expression

Discernment and expression concerns a principle in teaching basic skills and knowledge which is most important for all children. It refers to the main learning goals of the separate subjects as well as to the most fundamental psychological needs of young learners: to have the social world made meaningful, to comprehend, perceive and understand the purposes and contents of the learning activities, to gain insight into whatever knowledge is on offer and into the linguistic, logical, mathematical, artistic and technical operations and structures involved, and to give all one learns one's personal meaning by applying the taught skills and knowledge in expressions of thought, experience, questions, insights, feelings and fantasies. Thus, the principal teaching and learning objectives are at the same time the sources of what is called the internal motivation of the pupils.

This means that, right from the start, the learning of necessary technical, mechanical, formal and memorizing subskills have to be undertaken and framed by meaningful contexts, and directed towards principal goals like comprehension, understanding, communication and expression.

The relation between discernment and expression and the equality goal is twofold. Firstly, children from well-educated families usually acquire an orientation to basic skills at home. Hence, the detrimental and demotivating effect of an amputated curriculum is less harmful for them than for most working-class and immigrant children, who miss this self-evident preparation for learning at school. Therefore, a fully-fledged curriculum, ruled by the principal goals of learning, is doubly important for the motivation and scholastic achievements of disadvantaged children.

Secondly, in traditional educational practice, the reverse happens to be true. Usually, middle-class schools are the first to innovate with their curriculum in the direction of discernment and expression, while teachers in working-class schools more often show a strong tendency to contain discipline problems by restricting their teaching to meaningless routine subskills, which are easily checked and judged (Soutendijk 1973; Erp and Soutendijk 1973). This tendency clearly contributes to the reproduction of inequality by unequal educational investment of cultural capital.

Diversity of standards

Diversity of standards is an indispensable means to offer an alternative to meritocratic inequality. It can be viewed as an extension of discernment and expression, because it implies a broad and many-sided curriculum. At the same time, it represents a step to the participation objectives. According to Bourdieu's idea (1979; Collège de France 1985), diversifying the standards of judgement at school is seen as an alternative way to further equality in the 'now' and for 'later', namely by debilitating the apparent unidimensionality of the dominating middle-class rule and by enervating the social prejudices embedded in this measuring rod.

In the classroom, the introduction of a variety of standards has multiple effects. Individual children are not pinned to their failure any more, but are invited to show their success and are judged by other than only 'right or wrong' standards. Participation of pupils can be furthered directly. For example, in the Freinet way, when a group discusses the writings of pupils it can also develop a manifold of criteria to judge the qualities of a text. Collective emancipation effects can be strengthened by the introduction of standards which demonstrate the advantages of pupils from socially subdued or discriminated categories. For instance, the advantage of multilinguality can be demonstrated by the purposeful application in language or theme teaching of the abilities of immigrant children in speaking and writing their own tongue. The advantage of a musical home culture, which in general is better developed in most other ethnic groups than the Dutch, can be harnessed by using the diversity in musical traditions for the enrichment of music teaching at school. Or, there is the advantage of craft skills, which working-class parents can demonstrate at school by working with the pupils. And so on.

4. The framework explained: equality socialization

Co-operation

Co-operation is meant to replace 'hidden' competitive socialization in school with a conscious development of co-operative teaching, and thereby to prevent the production of discouraged losers which is inherent in the performance competition at school. Nowadays, we can find two main forms of performance competition in Dutch primary schools: the traditional and the modern.

The traditional way can be viewed like a high-jump contest. In the strictly grade-bound curriculum, uniformly taught to age-groups in the 'frontal classical' way, the bar is placed at the same height for every pupil in the classroom. Those who touch the bar are pushed back. For the pupils who at the end of the school year are still incapable of jumping over the bar, and therefore have to double the grade, the bar is at once placed a whole year's course lower. Thus, non-promoted pupils are absolute losers.

The modern way is more like a running race, although the rules can vary. It consists of several kinds of ability differentiation, which emerged under the influence of the individualization wave during the seventies and is ruled by the principle: each child according to its own pace and ability. Differentiation can be strictly individualized, which means that each child runs or creeps separately through the programmed courses. Frequently, the result is an unchecked lagging behind of 'slow learners'. Losing is a relative affair and can be mitigated by the way in which the teacher deals with it. Still, ambitious pupils, often pushed by their parents, can easily bring to the competition a collective awareness (by continuously comparing each other in how far one is, which number of the course cards one is working at, and the like), and thereby sharpen the notion of laggards as being the disqualified losers.

The other modern way is to let the pupils run in platoons by dividing them into groups of similar achievement levels by subject, within the classroom or across grades. In this case, losing is more overt and can result in transfer to a lower group.

The curricular and social effects of the various kinds of performance competition are partly different, but the overall result is the same: the losers, who have learned to be allergic to learning, are to be found mainly among the socially disadvantaged.

Co-operative education, especially in the area of basic courses, makes it possible to overcome the choice, which for many primary school teachers seems to be restricted to the traditional classical versus the modern ability grouping method.

Co-operation can be a unique way of bringing things together, because its purpose is manifold:

- to retain and strengthen the positive aspects of teaching in the classical way – its possible 'togetherness' – as well as in the differentiating way – its possibilities for adapting instruction, tasks and ways of learning to match the capacity, needs and problems of individual pupils;
- to twin these experiences with new possibilities, offered by collaboration and mutual help in mixed-ability or even mixed-age classroom groups or subgroups within the classroom and, thereby, consciously prevent 'hidden' competitive socialization;
- to make pupils acquire and train those social skills necessary for democratic communication and co-operation between persons at different kinds and levels of qualification and intellect, and from different (sub)cultures;
- thereby, to provide the pupils with the social tools to gain independence from the teacher and to create more equal relations between teaching adults and the taught children, who learn to teach one another;
- and to learn, from the beginning, the lesson that learning is a joint pursuit and that knowledge is a collective possession to be used for the common profit of everyone.

Although co-operative teaching and learning implies an emphasis on the collective activities of the whole class group as well as subgroups, it doesn't mean that 'formal classical' teaching and individual differentiation or temporary working with an ability group has to be abandoned. On the contrary, a purposeful varying of forms of teaching is needed to make learning at school less monotonous and more activating.

However, to make co-operation really serious, it should be geared to the development of effective co-operation and mutual help within mixed-ability groups of two to five pupils, working at group tasks on basic subjects. The positive equality effects, especially for multi-ethnic groups, of this specific co-operation are easily demonstrated. At the same time it opens the road to natural and non-stigmatizing ways of differentiation. Seemingly less able pupils appear to put the most fundamental questions about the subject matter in hand. Pupils, who in the competitive situation seem to be highly intelligent because of their rapid but superficial learning, are forced to think about the problems, and to learn to master subjects on a higher level by having to explain them to others.

Social integration

Social integration points to the aim of ensuring that all individual children and all categories of children belong, participate, and feel at home in the class and the school community; emotionally, socially and in their role as learners. Within the school environment, no child should be socially isolated, left-out, or banned from the group by teachers or by peers.

Social integration can be viewed as a central principle, which distinguishes the democratic approach from authoritarian and laissez-faire ways of teaching (cf. Anderson 1945; Lippit and White 1958). Creating a social integrative atmosphere also makes equality in the present, in the 'now', a necessary condition of school life.

The first requirement is respect for children, made concrete in the reversibility principle: teachers should consistently avoid saying and doing things to children which the children can't say or do in return without being cheeky, indiscreet, or impudent (cf. Tausch and Tausch 1965).

Secondly, it requires that teachers make children feel accepted as persons. Learning problems, 'bad' behaviour, language or performances, may never lead to the rejection of the child. Teachers should endeavour to stick to the original individualization aim. That is, to make room in their teaching for unconditional personal attention to the welfare, interests and problems of their pupils. Personal acceptance is a mutual process, which is furthered when the teacher consciously shows that she or he feels accepted by the children, by for instance, exposing her or his 'genuineness' through telling about her personal experiences or through showing his uncertainties.

It is by no means a spontaneous process. The teacher has to take the initiative. It appears often to be difficult to step over the 'natural' teacher's anxiety when in front of the pupils, to reach the freedom and confidence which is needed for laying down the façade of being the unfailing know-all without a personal life. And teachers should be aware of their natural human tendencies. The tendency to favour the 'good' and, thereby, mostly the socially privileged pupils in their personal attention (Thompson 1969); the tendency to engage in more elaborate talk about personal experiences, thoughts and questions of real life with those children who share a greater part of their social background and family experiences with the teacher, and who are usually not the working-class or immigrant children (cf. Tizzard and Hughes 1984).

Social integration has its connections with the other equality aims. That co-operation is an important means of furthering integration will be self-evident. Social integration needs the shaping of a tolerant and non-conformist classroom and school climate, which implies a consistent prevention of the 'natural' conformism of children in unsafe situations – a conformism which results in the scapegoating and rejection of individuals or minorities – of school- and playmates who don't wear the right clothes, don't use the right language, don't have the right hair or skin, don't see the right TV programmes, and so on. It will be clear that creating a tolerant climate has a tight connection with the introduction and employment of diversity of standards, and especially its emancipative application.

One peculiar source of rejection within the classroom situation consists of being a 'backward', 'stupid', or 'bad' pupil. This source will be more active when the teacher uses these labels in his or her public and comparative judgements of pupils. But notwithstanding the teacher's attitude, pupils will compare their attainments and judge each other's 'cleverness' as a personal trait, with stigmatizing, and thus social, consequences for 'slow learners', which negates the social integration aim. This is why social integration puts precise demands on the equal chances aim, and especially on the way achievement differentiation is used so that pupils who don't come up to particular minimum requirements receive extra, special attention.

Giving extra attention and didactical help to a subgroup of pupils with similar learning problems, for instance in a remedial teaching form or in the case of extra Dutch language lessons for immigrant children, should always be accompanied by measures aimed at further development of the social integration of these pupils in the classroom group. If not, the effect will be that possible learning gains are more than wiped out by an increase of the social problems of these pupils. So, for instance, extra assignments to overcome a particular subject-matter problem, should be so nice and attractive, so that these tasks can't be viewed as a punishment, not even by other pupils.

Equivalence

Equivalence concerns the furthering of virtual equality between categories of children in the 'now' of the school. The principle is an especially important way of considering the development of potentially racist or sexist relations in classroom and school.

The main explanation for the contradictory outcomes of the many American investigations in racially desegregated schools into their effects on interracial prejudices and relationships, appears to be the strategy of the school staff to further racial equivalence. With the absence of such a strategy, the unequal social relations between the races outside the school will be reproduced within the school, resulting in an increase of racist prejudice and discriminative attitudes and behaviour, contrary to the aims of desegregation (Schofield 1978). It means that the equivalence should be furthered by measures designed to promote the social status of socially subordinate groups within the daily educational practice.

An example can be found in one of our small-scale action-research projects which was carried out in the last grades of a multi-ethnic primary school. Some Moroccan and Turkish pupils showed stagnation in their acquisition of the Dutch language, which was coupled with a low status or even isolated position within the classroom group. Twice a week, these pupils got extra Dutch tuition in a separate group, especially directed to the acquisition of the linguistic and social skills of 'putting questions', according to a modification of Krashen's theory and method for second language acquisition (Krashen 1982; Krashen and Terrell 1983). The pupils were prepared not only to apply their learning in the classroom group, but moreover to take a leading role in language and question games within the framework of the collective theme-teaching. It resulted in a clearly increased popularity and higher social status of these pupils in the whole group according to sociometric measurements (Hezemans-Dirkmaat *et al*. 1984).

Equivalence through status-promotion can also be furthered by the emancipation application of diversity of standards. The enhancement of the social status of girls is usually effectively furthered by co-operative teaching and by stimulating the democratic initiatives of pupils themselves related to active participation and influence on the teaching and the daily course of events in school.

5. The framework explained: participation qualification

Extending the democratization framework to the participation goal, we meet a difficulty. We can't find examples of the development of an all-round participation-oriented education which accords with the equality objectives which we have in mind. At least not in common primary or secondary schools on a large scale. There is also little or no research available into the participation outcomes of democratizing schools. There are some experimental schools throughout Western Europe. Some of them are described in this book. Therefore, the greater part of our extension of the framework to *participation* can't be viewed as empirically grounded. We have to refer mainly to scattered experiences and 'philosophical' thinking.

As far as we can see, an emancipating *qualification*, geared to participation in the 'now' and for the 'future', should try to cover three elements: functional skills rooted in real life, critical knowledge and personal interests.

Real life and functional skills

Functional skills imply that the teaching of basic cultural skills (reading, writing, mathematics, information digestion, artistic and handicraft skills) takes place within meaningful contexts and emphasizes the active and creative usage (for personal and collective purposes) of the pupils themselves. To make this possible, the learning of basics has to be rooted in real life, as it is witnessed or explored by the pupils.

Real life is an unlimited concept. It refers to the challenge to make real for the pupils, what in traditional scholastic teaching remains verbal and abstract. There are many ways of bringing real life into school and into learning, or to bring the pupils out of the school to explore real life in the neighbourhood, the city, the farm, the harbour, the factory, the hospital, the zoo, the museum, and all the other places which many working-class and immigrant children won't witness during their schooltime if the school doesn't make the provisions for it.

According to the age of the pupils, the topics or themes and the ways to inquire and digest these experiences, will gradually change and be brought to a higher level. But real-life teaching will be based on the principle that the pupils are stimulated to participate by using and exchanging their personal experiences, and that of their families, about the real-life theme, which are used as starting-points in their collective inquiry and digestion of the theme. Real-life teaching will be enriched according to that range of social, cultural and historical experiences and knowledge, present in the school community and the classroom group, which is used in basic skill teaching and learning. Thus, the pupils will be able to profit from the advantage of belonging to a multi-ethnic school community. It supposes a positive appreciation of the diverse social, cultural and religious backgrounds of the pupils, their own language usage, their multi-linguality, their customs and artistic traditions.

The attachment of functional mastery of the basic skills to real-life teaching serves not only the participation goal, but, at the same time, acts as an important condition to further the equality aims. It furthers diversity of standards, it delivers the meaningful contexts for discernment, and it uses expression as an indispensable means.

Critical knowledge

Critical knowledge concerns making subject matter really universal by extending it to the experiences, knowledge, cultural achievements and history of both the oppressed and the dominating classes or groups, starting with those of the pupils themselves. It also means introducing information and knowledge which is produced by dissenting social and political movements. In this respect, teachers always risk being accused of 'indoctrination'. Viewed from a democratic standpoint, indoctrination is a very inconsistent and therefore unacceptable teaching method. But, actually, a great part of the commonly used textbooks and course materials contains a lot of overt or implicit information which consolidates the established order as well as white ethnocentric, sexist and classist prejudices. Hence, a 'neutral' teacher, who sticks to the textbook, is indoctrinating as well, albeit often unconsciously. Therefore, we should defend the right and even the duty of educators to make the sources of alternative knowledge available and accessible to the pupils to use and to debate.

Personal interests

Personal interests point to the individual side of emancipation. Participation not only concerns the liberation and uplift of oppressed groups, but also the winning of control over the arrangement of one's own life, according to one's personal view and preferences. This is not only a question of one's material and positional circumstances. It also depends strongly on the person's capacity to give sense to her or his life. A meaningful life supposes a vivid interest in some of the possible cultural activities a human being can be involved in during a lifetime. Education should stimulate the pupils to develop interests and qualify themselves for life. Therefore, the school should offer a wide range of possibilities in the arts, crafts, gardening, cooking, sports, and the like.

6. The framework explained: participation socialization

For the socialization side of the participation aim to operate supposes a conscious and active struggle for a democratic and emancipating pedagogy. Firstly, educators have to realize that children are one of the most powerless categories and therefore the most prone to oppression. A first device should be the removal of oppressive aspects of school pedagogy, as far as is possible. This does not imply an anti-authoritarian or *laissez-faire* approach, for it often requires consistent action from the teacher to make children learn not to oppress or cast out each other.

Equity and solidarity

Firstly, the purpose should be to bring pupils to a concrete understanding of the meaning of equity and solidarity by the practice of daily interaction and the gradual development of shared pupil control within the classroom and the school.

Equity means the extension of the legal principle of equal rights to the institutional and informal spheres, as opposed to institutional and everyday oppression of children. At the same time it means equivalence brought to awareness. A familiar, non-conformist and socially integrative school climate is the basic condition for meeting conflicts of interest (between pupils or pupils and teacher, or between different groups in the school). It makes it possible to turn real conflicts in classroom and school, which harm equity, into subjects for teaching and learning.

Solidarity of the socially privileged with the oppressed and the discriminated, and between different oppressed categories, constitutes the necessary complement of equity. To further develop solidarity is not only a socialization objective, but also aims to prevent the splintering of the group through conflict teaching. In order to make solidarity more than rhetoric, teaching should enhance the ability of pupils to take the perspectives of the disadvantaged, discriminated, or oppressed, by means of simulations, exchange of roles, real-life inquiry of discrimination, inviting popular persons who themselves experienced and fought oppression (cf. Bakker and Dorp 1985), undertaking collective actions against unfair situations in the neighbourhood, and the like.

Democratic skills

In order to develop and train democratic skills, our educational practice has to be directed to the development of shared pupils' control in the classroom and the school, and to their effective participation and influence in teaching school affairs. Always, this road will be gradual and complicated, paved by dilemmas and compromises. But without the intention of the school team and individual teachers to extend pupil influence and make small or bigger steps on this road, the pupils are denied even the smallest opportunity to learn from confrontations with other interests at stake, those of teachers, parents, and the authorities.

Actually, the development of participation, pupil influence, and the daily democratic functioning of the classroom group, will be more relevant for the pupils (and therefore for the learning of democratic skills) than the establishment of stationary pupil participation strategies at the school level, not only for young children, but also for teenagers. Without a minimal progress in pupil participation at the classroom level, pupil representatives in a school council lack a base, feel isolated, and are prone to manipulation by teachers and school management. Formal democracy, without a more direct pupil participation in the daily school and classroom life, can result in the 'reproduction' within the school of the same frustrated feelings against parliamentary democracy which 'common people' demonstrate in the society after school ends.

At both classroom and teaching levels, democratic pupil influence will always be an equivocal affair, ruled by dilemmas concerning the awkward relations between pupils' needs in the 'now' and learning objectives for the 'future', between the manifest influence of some pupils and the equivalence and equity among all pupils, and between pupil 'freedom' and the teacher's responsibilities. An important purpose of teaching democratic skills will be to reach a level of group functioning where these dilemmas are made public and subjected to open group discussion. In this way they are turned into instructive experiences in making democracy work.

It will be obvious that teachers can't abandon their responsibility for the process. They have to take the initiatives, they remain the goal keepers and those who guarantee the safety of each child. In every progressive step, they have to check and discuss the democratic rules about the ways pupils deal with each other in collective debate, decision-making and proposed action. That is because democratic skills suppose: a respect for minority rights and interests, and active striving for equal participation in discussions, decisions, planning and work load, obtaining experience with the exchange of leadership roles and the changeability and adaptability of those former democratic rules which have become dysfunctional. This process, in which pupils collectively challenge and gradually take over responsibilities from the legitimate authority of teachers, can be one of the most adequate ways of acquiring the skills and competence needed for an effective approach towards powerful people and authorities.

The existence of permanent classroom or basic groups of pupils during the school-year is an important condition for teaching democratic skills. Learning to live and work together and to consider each other's needs and wishes in a democratic way, (within the boundaries of compulsory education and the limited space, time and facilities) is certainly not a simple challenge, but it is a realistic one. The basic group is especially needed if one is to experience the principle of 'unity is strength', which represents an indispensable device for people from subordinate classes in their struggle for equal rights. Therefore, a hollowing-out and splintering of the basic groups can easily undermine the possibilities for co-operation and social integration as well as the learning of democratic skills.

Identity and autonomy

Identity and autonomy refer to the individualized objectives of socialization aimed at participation, just like personal interests refer to the qualification side. School is only a *part* of the child's life and even at school each pupil meets situations which she or he has to deal with alone, without the certainty of other people's support. This will be surely the case in society after school.

Therefore, the school should offer pupils the chance to gain independence and self-confidence, and to obtain the personal social skills which are needed in contacts with high-status figures, authorities, and the state bureaucracy. Personal strength in this respect is a necessary quality, which working-class children and girls have to acquire in order to develop and maintain their autonomy.

Autonomy means the mental freedom to choose your own social and cultural identity and live to it. Rich people can buy this freedom. Children from well-educated families, which belong to the dominating higher-middle-class culture, can easily reach their autonomy by simply sticking to their culturally distinctive background. Some persons attain autonomy through wisdom-based-on-knowledge.

When you lack the money and the dominating cultural background, and are taught at school that you are stupid, then you have to develop a very strong personality in order to gain personal autonomy.

Democratic education should support this struggle. Actually, it can be assumed that all other qualification and socialization objectives further autonomy, and that especially the participation objectives concerning functional and democratic skills and the development of personal interests contribute directly to it. Nevertheless, this won't be enough for many working-class children and certainly not for a majority of immigrant children. To gain autonomy, you should be able to digest consciously the social identity of your gender and social-class and ethnic group.

7. A central principle: publicity

One little oval in the centre of Figure 12.1 is left: publicity. It wasn't there in my original scheme. This concept was proposed by our Danish companions at the 1987 European Conference, and we recognized it at once as an important omission. This is because publicity was one of the most outstanding means used by the AIP (see Chapter 8 by Deckers and Van Erp in this volume) to stimulate the involvement and participation of all people concerned in the project at every level, from the pupils in the classroom to the Dutch Ministers for Education and for Welfare. As a matter of fact, we spent much energy and many activities on the furthering of publicity in all directions. Publicity between pupils, between teachers and pupils, between school and parents; between educational counsellors or action-researchers and the schools (concerned) and parents; between school and neighbourhood, (from schools to neighbourhood community to local authorities), demanding the same 'publicity' from 'them upstairs'. Publicity involves exchanges of relevant information, purposes, judgements and evaluations, products and opinions.

Democracy can't work without publicity. Therefore, it is put in the centre of the scheme as a central democratic principle in which the four fields are tied to each other.

References

Anderson, H.H. (1945). 'Studies in dominitative and social integrative behavior', *American Journal of Orthopsychiatry*, vol. 15, pp. 133–9.

Bakker, C. and Dorp, K. van (1985). 'Een Cubaans experiment. Kindersolidariteit, solidair word je niet geboren.' ('Solidarity of children, you are not born solidary' – about an experimental project of Mónica Sorin in Cuban primary schools.) *Vernieuwing*, vol. 44 (5), pp. 2–11.

Baudelot, Chr. and Establet, R. (1972). *L'Ecole capitaliste en France*. Paris, Maspero.

Bourdieu, P. (1979). *La distinction critique sociale du jugement*. Paris, Minuit.

Calcar, C. van (1980). *Innovatieprojekt Amsterdam. Eindverslag: een opening*. (The Amsterdam Innovation Project. Final report: an opening) Amsterdam, Van Gennep.

Collège de France (1985). *Propositions pour l'enseignement de l'avenir*. Paris.

Erp, M. van and Soutendijk, S. (1973). *Sociaal milieu en lesgebeuren. Een literatuur onderzoek*. (Social background and instructional process. An inquiry of research reports.) Amsterdam, Van Gennep.

Freinet, C. (1969). *Pour l'école du peuple*. Paris, Maspero.

Hezemans-Dirkmaat, M., Hülsenbeck, C. and Soutendijk, S. (1984). *Vragenderwijs. Een ontwikkelings-onderzoek naar gestuurde tweede taalverwerving binnen een thematische onderwijsaanpak*. (By the way of putting questions. An action research into guided second language acquisition within the framework of theme teaching.) Amsterdam, ABC.

Johnson, D.W., Maruyama, G., Johnson, R., Nelson, D. and Skon, L. (1981). 'Effects of co-operative, competitive and individual goal structures on achievement: a meta-analysis', *Psychological Bulletin*, vol. 89, pp. 47–82.

Krashen, S.D. (1982). *Principles and Practice in Second Language Acquisition*. Oxford, Pergamon.

Krashen, S.D. and Terrell, T.D. (1983). *The Natural Approach. Language Acquisition in the Classroom*. Oxford/San Francisco, Pergamon/Alemany.

Kreckel, R. (1976). 'Dimensions of social inequality. A conceptual analysis and theory of society', *Sociologische Gids*, vol. 23 (6), pp. 338–62.

Lippit, R. and White, R.K. (1958). 'An experimental study of leadership and group life', in E. Maccoby, T. Newcomb, and E. Hartley,, *Readings in Social Psychology*. Holt, Rinehart & Winston. New York, pp. 496–511.

Schofield, J.W. (1978). 'School desegregation and intergroup relations', in D. Bar-Tal and L. Saxe (eds), *Social Psychology of Education*. Washington DC, Hemisphere. pp. 329–63.

Soutendijk, S. (1973). *Het interaktiepatroon tijdens lessen in de tweede klas. Enschedese onderzoekingen in het lager onderwijs 1967–69*. (The interaction pattern during lessons in the second grade. The Enschede investigations in primary schools.) ISP, University of Utrecht.

Soutendijk, S. (1981). 'De rol van het onderwijs in de strijd voor maatschappelijke gelijkheid' ('The role of education in the struggle for social equality'), *Psychologie en Maatschappij*, vol. 14 (March), pp. 97–140.

Soutendijk, S. (1986a). 'Positieve aktie voor migranten jongeren' ('Positive action for immigrant children'), *Vernieuwing*, vol. 45 (6), pp. 15–21.

Soutendijk, S. (1986b). *Striptease van een valse boodschap, of hoe onderzoek aantoont dat demokraties baisonderwijs beter is*. (Striptease of a false message, or how research demonstrates the better results of democratic primary education.) Nijmegen/Amsterdam, ABOP/ABC/SOF/Vernieuwing/ WPRO. (An abridged English version is available from S. Soutendijk, Overtoom 321, 1054 JL Amsterdam.)

Soutendijk, S. (1988). *Understanding Democratization of Education: A Global View.* (The elaborated version of 'Equality and participation: the twofold goal of democratization'.) Amsterdam, Overtoon 321.

Tausch, R. and Tausch, A-M. (1965). *Erziehungpsychologie. Psychologische Vorgänge in Erziehung und Unterricht.* Göttingen, Verlag für Psychologie Dr. Hogrefe.

Thompson, J.M. (1969). 'The effect of pupils' characteristics upon pupil perception of the teacher', *Psychology in the Schools,* vol. 6 (2), pp. 206–11.

Tizzard, B. and Hughes, M. (1984). *Young Children Learning, Talking and Thinking at Home and at School.* London, Fontana.

Wesselingh, A. (1985). *Onderwijs en reproduktie van maatschappelijke onge-lijkheid 1975–1985.* (Education and reproduction of social inequality.) Nijmegen, OOMO-reeks, ITS.

Index

Compiled by Jackie McDermott